"Keep Quiet, You're Only A Girl"

"Keep Quiet, You're Only A Girl"

Gerry Di Gesu

iUniverse, Inc.
New York Lincoln Shanghai

"Keep Quiet, You're Only A Girl"

iUniverse, Inc.

For information address:
iUniverse, Inc.
2021 Pine Lake Road, Suite 100
Lincoln, NE 68512
www.iuniverse.com

ISBN: 0-595-31249-7

Printed in the United States of America

With love to Roger, Kevin, Christopher and Nancy
Thank you for being you

Contents

ACKNOWLEDGEMENTS

Unending thanks, love and appreciation to my husband, Roger, and my children Kevin, Christopher and Nancy for their constant love, inspiration and support through all my writing adventures. I am blessed.

Thank you Peter Saunders for helping me believe in myself and to friends and fellow writers in my Wednesday and Friday writing groups who provided companionship, acceptance and nurturance which enabled me to become the person I am today.

I found the anonymous quote appearing on the back cover many years ago and thank the author for words that provided validation and encouragement.

When there is light in the soul,
  there is beauty in the person.

When there is beauty in the person,
  there is harmony in the home.

When there is harmony in the home,
  there is honor in the nation.

When there is honor in the nation,
  there is peace in the world.

Chinese Proverb

INTRODUCTION

As soon as I could read, I fell in love with the mystery of books and their wonderful words and couldn't wait to tell my own stories. But as a child, all I remember being told was "Keep quiet; keep your mouth shut. Nice girls don't talk so much and no one's really interested in what you think anyway." I had lots of ideas and feelings to share but not even my parents or teachers wanted to listen to me. "Girls should be seen and not heard" was a mantra in the 1940s and 50s and I was born ten years too soon. Although I had many friends I still felt isolated and lonely, somehow on a different wave length. So I started to write. To me—for me—yet unaware that writing would become my lifeline......"Something regarded as indispensable for the maintaining or protection of life".

After lights out hidden under the covers with my flashlight, I spilled my heart and soul onto the tiny pages of a bright red diary. I recorded the joy, resentment and fears which I didn't even realize were part of me. Anger at my parents, a wild passion for the boy who lived across the street, fear that I wasn't perfect. Apparently aware of my hunger for words, my parents bought me a Smith-Corona portable typewriter for eighth grade graduation—the best gift I ever received. We became one.

I typed the summer away, nervously waiting to start high school. Hopes, ideas and dreams in a single-spaced stream filled sheets of legal-sized pages. In high school I had many friends and activities yet still felt like an outsider, an alien. Rarely did my views match popular opinion. Male teachers repeatedly told me to "sit down and keep quiet; you're only a girl". My typewriter remained my best friend, sharing the achievements, joys and heartaches of each day.

I married at twenty-one, raised three children and worked twenty-five years as a school secretary. Some essays were published in magazines and I had a weekly column in a few local newspapers during these years. But the hunger to devote my days to words never left. Scribbled notes, typewritten pages and stacks of journals were tossed into a huge box in my basement—waiting for someday.

At last, retirement and a move to Cape Cod, Massachusetts where I found refuge and where the beauty and order of nature helped bring balance and perspective to my writing. The opportunity to meet and share ideas with women writers was a wonderful and freeing experience. For the first time I no longer felt like an alien, the stranger looking in. These women tasted the joy of words I had always felt but never had been able to share.

Living alone without the obligations of home and family provided the luxury of daily writing. But more important, it gave me time and space for introspection and the chance to re-examine who I am. It's been a long haul but I finally like me.

I've walked the beach in all seasons, watched dragonflies hover magically over reeds in a pond, talked to a praying mantis on my knee and laughed at chickadees at the feeder. These fragmented sounds and images slowly developed into poems and essays. My husband and I have a new marriage, a new life. Days are full of joy. And I write.

Gerry Di Gesu
Union, NJ
January 2004

DREAMS

As a youngster it never occurred to me to think of myself as a wife and mother; I wanted to be a man. My mom went to work when I was thirteen and I shared many housekeeping duties since her health was frail and she needed help. I couldn't find one aspect of this role that appealed to me. I loved words and writing, not dusting, cooking and laundry. It seemed to me women had no choices in their lives and men had the world in their hands. I hoped to be Edward R. Murrow or Walter Cronkite, not a housewife. An important correspondent with a marvelous flair for words, I would help people understand their world. Or I imagined myself a respected journalist on an important daily newspaper, one day with Pulitzer Prize in hand. Dreams.

I read recently that in the 1950s approximately 5% of female high school graduates attended college. Only a few dozen girls in my graduating class of 300 were fortunate enough to enhance their lives through advanced education. The rest found a job, then a husband, had children and lived happily ever after. I desperately hoped to continue my education but my family couldn't afford it. My mother had gone to work to save for my brother's college tuition and "girls don't need school anyway" my dad said. So with a head full of dreams and vague plans for the future, I started work as a secretary in our local school system and met my future husband a month later. The rest, as they say, is history.

Unable to have children, we were married for six years when we adopted the first of our two sons and nine years later were blessed when I gave birth to our daughter. I loved my family like crazy and found the roles of wife and mother challenging, difficult and rewarding. But sharing daily conversation with neighborhood mothers proudly reporting on each step of potty training, making gingerbread houses or planning kids' birthday parties just wasn't me. I was a class mother for years until at one meeting this group of women took an entire afternoon to decide the appropriate icing color for holiday cookies. That's when I turned in my badge.

But guilt was a constant companion through the years since I felt there must be something terribly wrong with me when I couldn't share the total joy my friends seemed to relish in their roles as wife and mother. I yearned for a larger world and only books, an occasional writing course and public television filled that void.

I was always "writing in my head", making notes on the back of homework papers, on napkins from Dunkin Donuts where I found an idea or story each time I stopped for coffee, and on any scrap of paper available when the muses spoke. There was a large brown cardboard box in my basement which I filled with these notes, countless years of journals and an occasional essay, poem or story I managed to complete.

Now, forty years later, I've finally been able to open the box and find the first page of the rest of my life. I have glorious, endless amounts of time to write and will sign up for every course I want to take. I'm looking forward to Elderhostel to be my key to new adventures and new friends.

So—I'm not Edward R. Murrow. But I'm delighted to share these thoughts with you, and hey—when I win that Pulitzer you'll be able to say you knew me "when".

1997

BABE

When I first met my mother-in-law, I disapproved of almost everything about her. She smoked too much, talked too much, spent her money foolishly, murdered the English language and didn't take life seriously. Then slowly, over the years, without ever realizing it, this lovely woman taught me how to truly enjoy life. She taught me how to laugh.

Babe bounced through life, blonde curls swinging and blue eyes dancing. Widowed in her early thirties with three small children to raise, she survived on Social Security payments and guts, working at any job she could find and never complaining. Because her rent was raised often, she was forced to move many times in order to make a decent home for her children.

Over the years, she also suffered the ravages of two mastectomies. "If you've got it, you've got it, and there's nothing you can do about it," she said in her accepting way of the cancer that had invaded her body. "I guess that's what the Lord has planned for me." And then, with her usual zest and determination, she set out to put her life back in order once again. Any extra penny she had she shared with family and stranger alike. She worked long, difficult hours for low pay as a cashier in the neighborhood supermarket. She often came home upset over the bad luck one of her customers had suffered, determined to do something about it. She never mentioned her good deeds, but people would tell me how generous she had been to them. One woman who had been ill and had no money received Babe's brand new winter coat. "It was too small for me anyway," Babe said sheepishly. The free turkey she received each year from her employer always ended up on a needy family's Thanksgiving table. Household furnishings often found their way into the home of a struggling young couple.

On her day off she worked diligently to make her small apartment shine. Most of her furnishings were second-hand because that's what she could afford, but her gift for brightening her home was always evident in colorful pictures or knick-knacks obtained from garage sales. When she moved into a dank and dark first floor apartment behind an upholstery shop, I was devastated because it was all she could afford. I should have known better. In a few weeks fresh paint, starched curtains and her happy smile brought a glow to her new home.

Her back yard was comprised of a broken cement driveway and a row of sagging wooden garages which formed a buffer between the yard and the railroad tracks which ran behind them. But by summer she had transformed this soot-covered expanse into an oasis filled with wooden baskets crowded with prized tomato plants, glorious geraniums and mounds of brilliant petunias.

Everyone was welcome at Babe's home and most holidays were spent around a table covered with special treats she could ill afford. "I want to take good care of my stomach," she would laugh, patting her ample tummy. It didn't matter that she had used her weekly salary for this holiday feast—only that she could share it.

I used to think she was ignorant because she didn't know much about world events or politics, but the subjects just didn't interest her. "Can't do anything about what all those silly people want anyway," she grinned, "so why get excited?" She accepted people exactly as she found them without trying to change them. Seldom was she wrong in sizing up a new acquaintance or situation and she amazed me with astute perceptions and observations about human behavior. She just watched and listened.

We got to know each other better when she lived with me for a month when my daughter was born. Sitting on the porch in the warm fall sunshine, we shared hours of conversation. That's when I fully realized what a wonderful woman she truly was and how lucky I was to have her.

After she retired, she moved to senior citizen housing and enjoyed some of the happiest times of her life. Always ready for fun, she joined in all the activities with her usual gusto and was forever showing off new dance steps learned at weekly dancing lessons.

I'll never forget her grin as she splashed on perfume, fluffed her blonde curls and charged out the door dressed in a red, white and blue gown on her way to dance in a Busby Berkeley type of patriotic review at the senior center. I thank God she had those years of enjoyment free of the daily drudgery which had filled her life.

Babe died over twenty years ago but her legacy lives with me every day. A kind and beautiful lady taught me how to live and how to love.

AN EDUCATIONAL EXPERIENCE

There's only one rule to follow when tempted to provide children with an "educational experience". Don't. Leave them home, go by yourself and have a good time. A trip to the New York Museum of Natural History convinced me. I soon discovered that my two sons, eight and ten, were fascinated—by all the wrong things.

Although it was cool and comfortable at home, smog and exhaust fumes drifted in through the open car windows and choked us as we approached the Lincoln Tunnel. "You and your bright ideas", snarled my husband. "I told you this was a great day for fishing but you have to 'enrich our lives'. This should be some day." I ignored his tirade, but an uneasy feeling crept into my stomach. He might be right. Too many carefully planned outings had turned into disasters. This couldn't be another one.

After reaching the museum, the hardest part was getting the two boys as far as the front door. "Hey, Kevin. Come here. Please smile mister. Go on, keep smiling. Man that really looks great." Chris was grinning madly. The hot dog vendor near the entrance displayed a set of gleaming gold teeth that flashed brilliantly in the sunshine, entrancing my boys.

A swarm of bees joined us next, attracted to the containers of orange juice the boys were holding. One landed in the middle of Kevin's cup. "Hey, Chris. Look at this." Kevin swirled the cup rapidly. "Hey—only about thirty seconds. I timed it on my watch. That's how long it took for the bee to drown."

My "what makes it go" son soon discovered a floor-waxing machine, unfortunately still plugged in. "Ride em cowboy. Come on Chris hop on back and we'll ride double." They zoomed past startled visitors along the hallway who didn't seem to appreciate their equestrian skills.

While I waited for my family to return from the men's room, I desperately searched the directory for an exhibit that would interest them for more than five minutes. Kevin waltzed down the hall toward me, the front of his shirt wet.

"How did you get wet, Kev?" "Well I wanted to see why the urinal wasn't working and when I bent down daddy didn't see me."

Chris, the athletic eight year old, was oblivious to the twenty foot drop as he tried to hang by his legs from the balcony railing. Handrails in front of the display cases provided him with an excellent balance beam. A stern-faced guard rushed him back to me without comment.

The dark corners and huge showcases in the Hall of Indians provided the best spot for playing cowboys and Indians. An Iroquois Indian chant played in the background as my two Indians, using Kleenex at loincloths, gave their own rendition of a rain dance.

Sex. At last a display to hold their attention. Since the graphic descriptions of human anatomy recited by the boys recently led me to believe that Playboy was standard reading fare on the playground, I gulped and led them to a life-sized figure of a woman so I could explain reproduction. "Yuk", they yelled in unison. "She doesn't look like any of the pictures in daddy's magazines. Besides, we know all about babies and that stuff. Let's go see something interesting." I quickly steered them through a maze of huge, free-standing forms of iron, quartz and mica which were part of an extensive gem and mineral exhibit. We were headed for the front door. I had had enough.

The trip back to the Port Authority parking lot also proved to be educational. "Wow, she's really something," hollered Kevin as I dragged him gawking and grinning from a giant poster in front of an "art" movie. Too late, I realized we were on 42nd Street. The boys were amazed to discover that many skateboarders and bicyclists maneuvered through midtown traffic faster than taxis or cars. "He'll get a ticket," giggled Chris. It didn't faze him that the derelict sleeping in the gutter didn't belong there. Only that he was snoring loudly beneath a "No Parking" sign.

Home at last. Next time I'm tempted to educate kids, they'll learn about shore life and how to bait a hook. I'll soak up the sun and relax with a good book. My husband can fish.

1976

TWENTY-YEAR REUNION

"Why don't you kids leave me alone for a minute?" I leaned against the kitchen wall annoyed with the strident echo of my voice. If I wanted to make a good impression tonight I had to lower the octave a few notches and relax. I'd been twitchy as a cat all day. What was the big deal about a twentieth high school reunion anyway?

"Why do you want to go to one of those things?" grunted my friend Judy. "Everyone just sits around, looks over everybody else, finds out who has the best jobs and runs down those who aren't there. I was sorry I went to mine. It was such a bore." She dismissed me with a yawn.

I hadn't thought of it that way—only as a chance to see how far we had traveled over the years. Sure, it could be scary to realize how much time had passed, but it was a perfect chance to stop and reassess what we had done with our lives. My husband wasn't coming since he didn't know any of my classmates, so I was going with a friend from elementary school days.

How many would remember me? I seem to have a face that always reminds people of someone else but they never remember my name. My high school years had been happy ones but spent on the fringe of events, not really a member of that special popular group.

Although it was early when we arrived at the restaurant, a huge swirl of celebrants was already milling in the foyer. Two women on the reception committee greeted me. They had been class leaders, cheerleading captains and honor students. But time had diminished the sparkle in their eyes and even carefully applied makeup couldn't conceal the lines and furrows on their faces. I felt guilty at the thoughts that popped into my head and at the same time felt a satisfaction knowing I looked better than I did twenty years ago. Always the plain Jane, tomboy type, I had finally taken an interest in clothing and makeup—a "late bloomer". Now, along with the girls I had held in awe in my teens, I felt good about myself.

The dining room filled with a crush of people and the noise reached deafening proportions as we tried to out-shout and impress each other. Some people looked the same and others had a changed appearance which made them almost unrecognizable. We had our share of bankers, community leaders, doctors, an actress and a gregarious former cheerleader who now was a partner in a charter yacht company.

The most enjoyable conversations were with my buddies. I was always the one to whom they came for advice when they needed a date, when they wanted to know how to act with a girl or when they were trying to patch up a romance. If they only knew how often I had ached for them to ask me for a date instead of helping them solve their problems. What a delight to share the same easy camaraderie with them again.

Eddie—I remembered the gaudy rhinestone earrings and enameled pins snatched from his mother's jewelry box that he brought me as gifts when we were in sixth grade. He had put most obstacles in his own way but had learned to barrel through or climb over them. Now a successful businessman with a family, he was the one person I most enjoyed meeting again. Our long talk reassured me that he had come to terms with himself and life and the hardness in his eyes still belied the gentleness underneath as it always had.

Dinner was finished and the evening started to drag. After the usual "how are you doing, how many kids, where do you live, doesn't everyone look great" conversations, unless there were special memories to bind you that was the end of the conversation and it was time to move on.

Later I lay in bed, the word successful ringing in my ears as the faces of classmates danced before me. My family snored gently in their beds. My two sons are caring, giving teens and their sister is a delight to all of us. I'm sure to many tonight my husband's job in sales, my secretarial position and our middle-income routine life in the suburbs seems boring and stifled.

But I know over the years my family has worked hard and grown together into a solid, loving unit—not an easy accomplishment in today's society. The love my husband and I have for each other grows stronger each year. We are best friends.

With a smile, I roll over to sleep peacefully, satisfied that I'm a "successful" graduate.

6-7-77

LIFE

My parents are buried in this cemetery and I have stopped to visit and seek help from them. To try to be as brave coping with life every day as they were when they faced death—perhaps a selfish reason. I come not because they rest here, but because I'm empty and need to try and draw upon their strength to help myself.

It was often difficult to approach them for support through the years because it seemed to me that they weren't emotionally strong enough or able to understand and support me and my many needs. Then I watched as they faced death and discovered two people I had never known before. Never self-pitying or complaining, they had shown their true inner strength as they battled the ravages of the cancers which claimed them. Now I needed them to share their fortitude with me.

Standing over the double grave, I look at the ground but no picture forms in my mind. I don't think of them being here, don't feel sad. I know they're watching me, happy and content. It seems as if they left me yesterday and then again an endless number of years ago.

The groundskeepers have mistakenly placed the Christmas blanket of balsam and fir on my grandmother's adjacent grave. I try to move it but it's anchored securely to the ground and I can't budge it. "Heck" my dad would say. "I don't care about any fancy decorations. Bring me a good healthy tomato plant in the spring instead."

This is the first time I notice many elderly people visiting the graves of their loved ones for the holiday season. One woman supports an old man who shuffles along and clutches a handkerchief to his face. I ache for him. Strange, but I feel more sorrow and emptiness for the visitors than I do for my parents or myself.

The biting wind forces me back to the car. On my way toward the exit gates, I pass a small wooden bridge with a partially frozen stream flowing sluggishly beneath it. The sight of two trees on the opposite bank startles me, forcing me to stop the car.

It appears that the cemetery workers have decorated the twisted branches with yellow Christmas ornaments, uniform in size and crowding the boughs. Blazing and gleaming in the brittle yellow light, the balls bounce furiously in the bitter wind.

I know it's ridiculous to assume the trees have been decorated and get out of the car to satisfy my curiosity. Shriveled golden crabapples are clustered on the branches. I pull one from the tree, amazed that the vicious wind has not yet torn it from the branch. Further along the creek bed two smaller trees sway in the wind, their golden fruit sparkling with life.

I realize that God is sharing these golden balls which clutch tenaciously to the branches as a reminder that there is brightness, life and hope after death. To give reassurance in these sad surroundings.

I wipe my cheek and smell the balsam that clings to my glove, a gentle reminder that my parents and their strength will always be part of me.

HAPPY NEW YEAR

For the past two weeks I've been trying to write a New Year's column without success and can't understand why. I feel at loose ends, unfocused; what do I want to say? Many of us suffer from post-holiday letdown; everyone seems to be sick and unable to shake off whatever bug has invaded their system. It's a downer.

My holidays were peaceful, happy and uncomplicated but I felt no joy. At first I thought it was me, but many people I talked to, including teenagers, seemed to share the same feeling. Not particularly rushed or harried, but empty, a void, ennui hard to shake off. Christmas seemed to be a big chore to get through, another job done. A sad commentary on a festive season.

I've come to the conclusion that part of this feeling comes from possessing too many "things". We suffer from the poverty of plenty. Christmas presents often only add to a surplus of already unused or under-utilized items cluttering our lives. I realize there are many who don't have enough to meet even the basic costs of food, shelter and clothing, but many of us are able to buy whatever we want. The problem is, things don't seem to make us happy; otherwise, why do we always want more?

Someone will always have more expensive jewelry, a bigger home, a larger income, two SUVs instead of one, smarter kids or a connection enabling them to get the promotion we deserve. Why can't we ever be happy with who we are and where we are?

So my wish for you this year is for less. Especially paying less attention to undefined "shoulds" and what "they say" and listening to your own inner needs and desires for a change. Less racing around on roads which become more congested by the day. What's the rush? Instead of hunching over the wheel, blasting the horn and swearing, sit back and relax. You'll get here just as fast.

If you're tired after coaching Little League for years, had enough of being a Brownie leader, or given all the time you can or want to give to an organization just say "sorry, I'm tired". To kids who often make unreasonable and selfish demands on your time it's ok to say: "Not today, I have something I want to do." They'll survive and hopefully learn the give-and-take of a healthy family and society.

My fondest wish is for less television, video games, MTV and sexual and violent films. The media message of hype, noise and competition assaults our senses and sensibilities, insidiously working its way to the core of our being. And we wonder why we're always running, hyper or hostile. Maybe because it's expected and accepted.

And for next Christmas season: fewer gifts for folks on your list, perhaps just one, even for family members. But a gift you've selected with love and care, not a check-off item on a list. Less to eat and drink. Less holiday hassle by celebrating the way you want to, not the way they say it should be done, whoever your particular "they" may be.

Try less this year. It gives you more of a chance to be you.

1985

BROOKLYN DODGERS

October 8, 1957—"Brooklyn Dodgers moving to Los Angeles" was the headline in all New York City papers that day. There had been talk since spring training that the team would move out of Brooklyn because New York (whoever that was) wouldn't give the Dodgers permission to build a new stadium. But I knew they would never leave. My bums, the perennial underdog, had finally won their first World Series in 1955 and would play at Ebbets Field forever.

My dad had been a pitcher on a Triple A baseball team and dreamed of making it to the big leagues, a dream which never came true. He loved all sports. Since my brother, who was two years younger, wasn't interested in sports at all, I became dad's buddy. The main thing I remember as a kid was always being with my dad either tossing a football, shooting baskets or improving my pitching and batting skills. We spent the spring and summer following golfers around the local 18-hole golf course, attended every baseball and softball game in town leagues and watched the Giants and Dodgers on television.

I was an excellent athlete, usually the captain of our school or playground team. From grammar school until high school graduation, most of the time I had first choice of whom to pick for my team. I loved to win, yet at the same time sensed the need of kids who weren't good at sports to be included. From a young age I always championed the underdog, whether in sports or in life and felt I could help kids gain confidence through athletics. I was determined to become a physical education teacher and coach.

By the time I was eighteen and graduated from high school, I was so idealistic I knew that life and people would be kind and fair. And I knew everything. That's how I knew the Dodgers would never leave Brooklyn.

Throughout the season I read the sports pages every day, trying to understand the reasoning of people who would ask a team which was the soul of a community to move and leave thousands of loyal fans with broken hearts. My dad tried to explain the politics, the economics and the egos of the decision-makers. But I wouldn't believe what I read or what he told me. It wouldn't be fair—to anyone. And I knew that couldn't happen.

On October 8, 1957, when I realized the Dodgers were really going to leave, it became a seminal point in my life—innocence lost. It was the first time I realized life would not be fair, people would not be kind or care about others, money was a corruptive symbol of control and power and—I didn't know as much as I thought.

RISK

Chris, who is twenty-two and one of my adopted sons, met his biological mother a few weeks ago and it was one of the most joyful days of my life. For reasons I don't fully understand the idea of adoption still carries a mystique and often a negative connotation for many people. That's why I want to share my joy with you.

When I mentioned to close friends that my son was being sought by his birth mother, I was surprised to find that the majority assumed I would feel threatened and fearful when actually I was delighted. I cannot imagine being either the mother of a child given up for adoption who never knows what happens to her child, or being the adoptee who goes through life not knowing his background and who he really is.

My husband and I had told Chris and Kevin, twenty-four, that we would help them find their biological parents but that they had to realize it could be either a wonderful or a traumatic, upsetting experience, depending on the person they found.

I realized Chris' meeting could go either way, but the fact that this woman had waited until he was twenty-two to inquire about him so she wouldn't disrupt his family gave me good vibes about her. Chris' easy acceptance of her invitation and his attitude convinced me he was sound and prepared to cope with whatever he might find.

After initial separate interviews with the social worker at the agency who had made the placement, Chris and his birth mother met at the agency office. I was a wreck the whole day, watching the clock, trying to imagine the emotions in that room.

I arrived home from work just as he returned home and had a million questions for him but didn't want to crowd him because I knew he must be a swirl of conflicting emotions. He had to rush out to work but asked if she could come to our home and meet the family later in the evening. Of course we said yes; I was dying to meet her.

Later, I opened my front door to greet a bright and smiling woman whose sparkling eyes reflected the joy of her day. We hugged and cried and then sat down with the rest of my family to get acquainted. Tentatively, we felt our way around each other, not wanting to pry but wanting to know everything. What I remember most was the constant sound of laughter in our living room that night.

Calmly and without self-pity she shared her story, relating the callous and harsh treatment she received from her family, the social agency and hospital staff, none ready to offer understanding or compassion to a scared young teen. She explained how desperately she wanted to keep her baby and only at the last minute, when she realized there was no hope of caring for him, she signed the adoption papers.

She had been terrified to return to the agency for help in finding Chris, expecting the same harsh treatment, only to be delightfully surprised to find warmth and empathy instead. She battled the constant fear that neither my son nor his family would want to meet or accept her. How I admired her courage as she risked rejection each step of the way on her search for her child. At last we finally said goodnight. I felt happy knowing I had a new friend and that Chris knew who he was and how much he was wanted.

Time will tell how this relationship will develop but I know that the look on my son's face and the joy in this woman's eyes as they said goodbye and she hugged him for the first time reinforced my belief that we can't be afraid—we have to risk and reach out in love.

1990

A DAY OFF

"Come on, mommy, I can take care of you. Please get up." The gentle tapping on my shoulder grew more insistent. I turned in bed to face my grinning daughter. She was absent from her kindergarten class with a lingering cold and I was nursing a case of laziness. "Ok, hon. Let's go down and make a cup of tea." Today the mess I passed through in the living room didn't faze me. Newspapers, books and snack plates were piled in the corner. Someone else could pick them up later. The thought of piled up laundry and empty grocery cabinets didn't upset me either. I didn't feel like doing anything.

I turned on the gas under the tea kettle when the phone rang. The last thing I wanted to do was chat but remembered someone might be sick and need a ride home from school. My son's guidance counselor was calling to confirm an appointment. "You're dresser drawer is messy, mommy. Can I clean it out?" Oh, no. Nancy had been investigating while I was on the phone. My usual reaction would be a curt "stay out of my room" but it was a junk drawer and she was careful and considerate.

"Sure, honey, go ahead and have fun." Her blue eyes sparkled and I got a big squeeze. I flopped down on the kitchen chair with my tea and opened the morning paper. A long time passed before she reappeared.

"I got all dressed up, mommy. Don't I look pretty?" Attired in a Raggedy Ann sweatshirt and red jeans, she had somehow managed to wiggle her blue flowered bathing suit on over them. Two strands of multicolored beads hung from her neck to her knees and she clopped along in white, furry snow boots. "And mommy, how do you like my eyes?" She had found glittery blue eyeshadow and applied it deftly. She sparkled and smelled good. Perfume. My daughter would be feminine in spite of me.

She disappeared down the cellar stairs and I cleaned up the kitchen. "This is Chris' old paint-by-number picture and he didn't finish it. Can I?" Again tempted to say no, I thought—what's the difference. It would only get thrown out eventually. "Go ahead and finish it honey but bring it up here." She brought up the picture and set it on the kitchen table. Soon she was blobbing colors together, swirling her brush around and singing loudly as she worked. "Aren't I doing a good job, mommy? This is so much fun," she bubbled.

It was delightful to just sit and watch her. Why was I always too busy? Doing what? Going to meetings, Boy Scouts, conferences. Was all the running really necessary? I try to spend some time with each of my children every day but never seem to find or make time. Now my boys are in their teens and I was afraid they would share little of their feelings with me in the future. I couldn't let my daughter slip away because I was too busy to listen.

I watched her, fascinated by the changing expressions on her face as she worked diligently, experimenting with colors and shapes on the paper. "I'm done, mommy. Isn't it beautiful? I'll put it on the table for daddy so he can see it when he gets home."

The bright family room looked warm and inviting as I passed the doorway. An unseasonably warm day with brilliant sunshine streaming in provided us with a perfect spot for lunch. With little direction Nancy made sandwiches, bustling around the kitchen, feeling important and gaining self-confidence. This time I didn't stop her with "hurry up; I'll do it myself".

We watched the squirrels repair their nest in the birch tree. Gray tails twitching, they put on an acrobatic show for us, jumping from tree to tree, bobbing on the springy branches and stealing their lunch from the bird feeder. "Why do their tails wiggle? Why don't they fall off the branches? How do they keep warm?" I had time to answer the questions that tumbled from my daughter.

Our backyard abuts a cemetery and a funeral procession had entered and stopped down the road where we could see the mourners through the trees. I tried to answer Nancy's questions about death, hoping that my answers would convey my belief that death is a continuation of life and nothing to fear and that God was her best friend. She seemed satisfied and snuggled closer.

"I feel tired mommy. Let's take our nap now." We burrowed down on the couch; the warm afternoon sun provided a blanket for us. I hugged Nancy to me. Not tomorrow. Today was the day to enjoy my daughter.

1979

CLUTTER

Clutter can tell you a lot about life. Yesterday I started to scoop up the mess on my dining room table wondering how it piled up so fast and how to prevent it from accumulating practically overnight. Then I stopped to take a closer look and discovered a marvelous collection of success stories.

A letter and photographs from friends who moved to Maine last fall. They hated living in New Jersey, the rat race, pollution, noise and going to work each day. So they sold their home and off they went with their two young children, little money, no job prospects and joyous hearts. I still think they're crazy but when I read their letters describing how happy they are out in the woods, I envy their free spirit and wonder if perhaps they don't have the right idea.

A thank you note from a friend to whom we had sent a gift when he opened his own beauty salon last month. I can remember him growing up always talking about owning his own business. He had worked long, grueling hours for years to save the money to succeed and now his dream had come true

My son's homework and test papers for the last few weeks, all with excellent grades. We had encouraged, nagged and punished during the previous months and now here was proof that he is starting to realize his potential and grow in self-confidence. I know he's on his way.

A Bible, banner and huge, hand-drawn poster of St. Matthew brought home by my teenage son from a Crossroads Catholic weekend retreat. I will never forget the joy and exuberance of the forty boys and their families as we said welcome back to them in the church hall. One after the other they rose to share their deepest feelings about God with us and say, "Thanks mom and dad. I love you." I wonder how many parents heard those words for the first time that night.

Copies of minutes from a learning disabilities organization meeting. The untiring, selfless years spent by the founder of this group to help the children and their families. Professionals I've dealt with over the years who were trying to help my son, all of them caring people. He's come a million miles because of them.

In the center of the table rests a painting of daisies in delicate water colors. It arrived in the mail today, a gift from a friend from high school days. A sensitive, caring woman who wanted more than anything to become a successful artist. We lost touch over the years and I learned she had been assaulted by divorce, the death of a child and a drinking problem.

The letter that accompanied her painting announced her one-woman show at a prestigious California gallery and left no doubt my friend had won a long, hard battle. My answering note will offer congratulations on her upcoming exhibit, but more than that will share her joy in becoming one of life's survivors.

1979

REFLECTION

It's one a.m. My favorite time of the day. Silence. The doorbell and phone have stopped ringing; the television rests. No one calls "ma". I can hear my home around me. The refrigerator shutters to a stop; the furnace clicks off; the cuckoo clock tells me I better get to bed.

I turn off the lights and in the darkness open the front door to see if promised snow has started to fall. The snow hangs heavy in the damp air, muffling all sound, ready to drop its first flakes in a moment.

Two quarters clink in my bathrobe pocket as the tooth fairy gropes her way upstairs into her daughter's bedroom. I reach under her pillow, searching for the tiny calico tooth holder in which she has proudly set her front tooth for pickup. I exchange my quarters for her tooth and as I listen to her gentle snoring am again reminded of the joy this youngest, unexpected child brings to our family.

I open the door and peer at my two teenage sons. It's just nice to look at them, love them and say a silent "sorry" for being an unreasonable witch today. The older one sleeps quietly with no sign of the wracking cough and asthma that kept him awake through the night for years. I whisper a thank you to the allergist who has brought him this far. My younger son is talking excitedly in his sleep, replaying an afternoon football game. His body might be quiet but his mind never rests.

The click of the electric blanket assures me of another toasty night as I slip into bed. The wind grows stronger. Is it snowing yet? I burrow deeper into the covers. Sirens scream on emergency vehicles racing toward the nearby hospital and it's good to know my family is safe. Neighbors slam a car door, laughing loudly.

The roar of a jet overhead. Where is it headed? How many nights I've heard the same roar and wished I was aboard—bound for anywhere. To be able to run away—from family, responsibilities, problems. But that's on the bad days. Today was a pretty good one.

My husband's even breathing annoys me and I want to give him a nudge just to be nasty. How can he sleep so peacefully after the noisy, upsetting argument we had. He insulted me and then charged off to bed without a word. I draw away from him but then remember my friend, widowed recently, who aches to be able to reach out and touch her husband again.

I lean over and give my husband a gentle kiss on the cheek. Now I can sleep.

1980

DINING ROOM TABLES

When we moved into our home, I was determined to have a lovely dining room which resembled the layouts in glossy decorator magazines. Seventeen years later, I'm still waiting. Unfortunately the only passage from our living room to the kitchen is through the dining room, so this middle room has become a catchall. I've tried using bright tablecloths and seasonal centerpieces as focal points but now school books, footballs and piles of junk mail cover the tabletop instead.

We bought our set second-hand right before we moved in and figured it would serve our needs for a few years while the kids were young. Now I think it will probably still be here when my grandchildren arrive. I'd love to have a new set but every time I see another chunk out of the sideboard I'm happy it isn't a piece gouged from the cherry Queen Anne set I yearn for.

On rainy days when the kids were toddlers, the table provided a great place for fun. A few old sheets thrown over the sides quickly transformed it into a fort, spaceship or castle. It was also a perfect hiding place for them to avoid detection or punishment. They would stretch out on two chair seats beneath the table and, hidden by the tablecloth, quickly disappear from sight.

The boys discovered a shelf under one end which they used for storage, a hiding place for forbidden gum and candy, baseball cards and various pieces of broken toys I wasn't supposed to find. Some of the items stashed away can't be mentioned but at least nothing alive or furry ever crawled out to greet me.

The tabletop is an excellent launching site. Books, papers and gym bags are piled in a corner ready for school; sleeping bags, knapsacks and boxes of food stand ready for a Boy Scout camping trip. In the spring a tackle box, fishing poles, reels and seasick pills line the table awaiting the next day's fishing expedition. Countless numbers of Girl Scout cookie orders were filled from this spot; Christmas presents wrapped and Halloween candy sorted and catalogued. Many frustrating yet happy hours were spent at the table trying to complete a paper mache' volcano or mountain range for social studies class.

The table also serves as a spot to change play clothes or diapers of visiting toddlers who always seem to be getting into something messy. There's plenty of room to attend to bloody noses, clean scraped knees or share the hugs that make everything better.

Yes, we do eat at the table and it's this sharing that evokes the warmest images and memories—special birthday parties and family celebrations; Thanksgiving and Christmas dinners with all of us scrunched together but full of joy; steaming crabs tossed onto newspapers covering the table to accompany shrimp and lobster when we could still afford such a feast. A special feeling of closeness with members of a church discussion group as we learned to share complex and sometimes controversial ideas and feelings. The memories of the smiles, faces and voices of loved ones as they sat around the table who are no longer here—not sad memories but images which fill me with gratitude and delight. I guess we probably won't replace this set after all. I could never replace the memories.

1985

A BEACH DAY

It had to be a good day. We were headed for my favorite spot—the beach—to spend the day with a friend and her family at their cottage. The omens were good: a cloudless sky, the air clear and cool and the Garden State Parkway surprisingly uncrowded.

Arriving early to cram as much activity into the day as possible, we quickly unloaded shovels, rafts and everything else kids need for the beach. The first thing the boys did was upset the picnic cooler and dump our lunch—sand for the sandwiches. I could taste the salt on my lips and the warm sun soaked into my bones as we headed across the sand. The kids charged at the ocean and the week's problems slipped away.

Fishing boats were anchored close to shore but more fishermen seemed occupied with eating or drinking since not too many were reeling in fish. Countless party and pleasure boats jockeyed for position in the shallow water. Kites competed with seagulls for airspace. Fierce dragon faces filled the sky and multicolored box kites, tails drifting behind them, danced overhead. A few homemade contraptions proudly soared closer to the sun than sleek kites bought on the board walk.

It was quiet on the beach. Hammered by noise all the time, it wasn't until after I reached home that I realized how peaceful it had been loafing on the sand. Not one portable radio blared rock or the ball scores; no recorded music assailed us from the boardwalk. Nice sounds: waves crashing, kids squealing, folks laughing—people having fun.

A group of beach-blanket Romeos next to us displayed an amazing ability to change approach and tactics instantly as each girl passed by. Raised eyebrows, suppressed smiles, a cool stare—all seemed to elicit the same response from the parading beauties—disdain. One boy described a chunky, bikini-clad girl as having "MGTB". More guts than brains.

The ocean was gentle, warm and I hope clean. My kids shared my joy in the foaming, salty water. Frightened looks disappeared and clutching grasps loosened as they bounced over the waves. Soon they were laughing and splashing like pros.

When a wave dumped them they surfaced, spitting sand and looking bewildered, but charged right back for more.

Tired and sunburned, my friend and I took a leisurely stroll back to her bungalow and reminisced about experiences shared through the years. Although we often don't see each other for months, the sharing of joy, heartaches, hopes and disappointments has cemented a lasting friendship. With a friend, time makes no difference. I reached out to give her a hug and "thanks for the great day" but drew back, remembering she is not a toucher. Her wink and smile told me she shared the same feelings.

Once we showered it was time to head for home. Three wilted kids battled for awhile but a change in seating quieted everyone. They were too tired to fight. Approaching the Raritan River Bridge, my eyes smarted and my throat tightened as the haze and pollution from the factories along the river seeped into the car. It always angers me, riding over that bridge and being exposed to such a mess. But then a thought came to me: hey, maybe someday we might clean up this pollution. And you know, I believed it. It was that kind of day.

1980

OVERHEARD

In the course of baby-sitting for my two granddaughters, eight and eleven, while their mom recovered from surgery last week, I drove them to and from school—a forty-mile round trip daily. The weather was mild so each day I got to school early for pick-up and waited on the playground with young moms for the children to come out of school. An education. We haven't "Come A Long Way Baby".

I love to watch and listen to people; it's the best education on earth. But I was surprised and dismayed that the conversations of many of these young mothers were exactly the same as those I heard on the playground over twenty years ago when my daughter started kindergarten. Most of the mothers looked haggard for their age, worked either full or part-time and were annoyed because they had two jobs, put in long days and complained they got little support or help from their husbands. Many of them "couldn't be who I truly am" because they were busy pleasing parents, husbands and children. I was amazed. That's where I was a million years ago. What happened to women's lib and equal opportunity and........?

After listening to these women for a week, I felt as if I knew them individually. They weren't feeling sorry for themselves but were expressing genuine frustration and confusion, trying to find ways to cope with their multiple roles and raise children in our increasingly complex society.

The following week at a Mc Donald's on the Connecticut Turnpike on my way back to Cape Cod from New Jersey, I took a seat in a booth with my back to two men who appeared to be in their thirties who were talking loudly. One man did most of the talking and he was upset, hurt and angry. Why? Because he couldn't follow his heart and had to do the "guy thing, you know" as he said to his friend. I have never heard a man speak so candidly about love, pain and relationships. He even said to his friend, "I can't believe I'm telling you this because guys aren't supposed to talk this way".

It was a long conversation regarding a woman he loved deeply who apparently shared the same feelings for him. The tragedy was that over and over, through the variety of scenarios he described, he couldn't allow her to see how much he loved her. He wanted to hug her kids but was afraid to, couldn't talk to his own dad about his pain and didn't know what to do with his feelings. He kept repeating, "It's not macho, you know, it's not a guy thing. It's not what guys are supposed to think and feel. We're supposed to be cool." Soon they left and I felt deep sadness as I watched them pull away.

I pulled out onto I-95 and started thinking about the two men I'd just heard and the group of women I had listened to during the last week. And then I thought about our super-speed technological age where everyone has instant access to everyone else through the wizardry of electronics. The contrast was stark. Men and women can talk to each other within seconds today. But how many of them are sadly still stuck in stereotypical roles within our society and don't know what to say?

Fall 2000

CHRISTMAS CONFUSION

"Hey, hon, here's a great recipe for Christmas cookies." Oh, no. I clatter the dishes louder in the sink and pretend I don't hear my husband. He has Christmas on his mind and that's bad. He's just not realistic when it comes to planning holiday gatherings. He thinks that he—the perfectionist—and I—the klutz—and our three young kids can spend Christmas in the following manner: our home will resemble decorating themes from Colonial Homes, my baking will put Martha Stewart to shame and our entertainment ideas will be featured in Gourmet Magazine. Actually, the way we spend our holidays is more like Saturday Night Live.

Take presents. My husband likes surprises; I don't. An unappreciated portrait of George Washington has stared dolefully at us from over the mantle for many years because Roger admired it in a furniture store and I surprised him. New ice skates wait patiently in the attic for five years for the man who couldn't wait to go skating with his family. So much for surprises. Choosing presents is difficult but wrapping them is worse. His meticulously wrapped gifts look as if they came directly from gift wrap. I possess ten thumbs, none of which ties bows, but I'm an expert at piecing. My main talent consists of being able to fill in the spaces with extra paper after I've misjudged and cut another piece of gift wrap not quite large enough to cover the entire package.

Rod is artistic and creative; I have trouble duplicating stick figures. His wreath on the front door must measure 6 and 7/8 inches down from the top because that's exactly where it belongs. I search for the smallest tack hole left over from last year and hammer away. He never realized I cut off branches from our front hedge to fill in bare spots in the wreath after the kids partially destroyed it last year. He neatly winds and trims yards of ribbon through the spindles and banister leading upstairs. I cut off the edges or cram them under the carpeting on the stairs where they're hidden—just as easy, twice as fast. I usually let the kids decorate the tree. So what if there are four gingerbread men on one branch; it fills in. Rod prefers a three inch space between gingerbread men, coordination among the bright rocking horses, wooden soldiers and toy drums—not too many candy canes near the top, watch out for the lights…..and on and on.

"Company's here." In the kitchen I sneak a huge gulp of Chianti hidden in my yellow Mc Donald's cup to fortify myself against the onslaught of relatives. After everyone is hugged, kissed and settled, we exchange presents and trouble begins. Cousin Jane has a pinched look on her face since she's sure her bracelet cost less than the one I gave to my aunt. The kids get wilder and my head starts to ache.

Rod gives me a disapproving look because I'm wearing slacks and summer sandals. He's annoyed that I'm not attired in the loose, flowing hostess outfit he bought me. But I'm not a loose, flowing hostess and the sandals are for safety. Last time I wore something "flowing", the sleeve caught on a chair, I slipped, and a river of rich brown gravy flowed across the dining room rug. I'll look glamorous if he cooks.

I suggested a buffet since our dining room is too small to accommodate the sixteen of us who gather each year. Rod was horrified. We must have a sit-down dinner. He spent the entire food budget on assorted snacks, cheeses and wine. When it was time to "sit down for dinner" no one could move. They were stuffed and I wanted to kill. So we ate ham for two weeks.

"We'll never have them all here for Christmas again" my husband says with a groan. "It's just too much and the kids drive me crazy." I've heard the same refrain on Christmas night for the past ten years. As I hand him two aspirins, I notice he's tearing out a page of recipes from Woman's Day to file away. He's already planning next year's menu.

December 1980

THUNDERSTORMS

Working at the sink by my kitchen window, I sense a change outside. Trees that ruffled gently all day stand motionless. The birds are still. Black clouds are piling up in the west. I set aside my pots and hurry out the back door not wanting to miss a minute of the approaching storm.

Ever since I was a child I've loved thunderstorms. I would lie on the porch glider waiting eagerly for the approaching storm to arrive with its kaleidoscope of color and sound, retreating only when I became soaked by needles of rain.

Sparrows are perched in a row on the telephone line—silent, waiting. I always wonder where they hide to escape the wild winds and driving rain. So small and vulnerable, yet they are the first to reappear happy and chirping after the rain subsides. Other times, as a storm approaches, the yard is filled with wildly chattering birds. Is their decibel level somehow an indication of how severe a storm will be?

Within minutes the sun is hidden behind massive clouds and the breeze twists the leaves on their stems. My yard is bathed in a strange yellow-green light that makes me feel like an adventurer traveling toward the unknown. The sky quickly turns from gray to black; the wind roars through trees which have formed a wind tunnel and the first huge drops pelt down on my head.

My sons fly into the house complaining that their baseball game is ruined. I hurry them off to shut the windows as fast as possible. My daughter clings to me as two claps of thunder shake the house. We go out onto the enclosed porch where we can enjoy the full fury of the storm and help overcome her fears.

Sheets of rain slam against the glass, the clump birch whip wildly; the low spot in the yard quickly becomes a lake. Nancy starts to cry; she's afraid her daddy's tomato plants will be broken. A quick check out the dining room window reassures her that most will stand straight once the deluge stops.

The driving rain slows to a steady drizzle and I'm disappointed. I like it when the storm stops as suddenly as it starts. Mother Nature must read my mind for the sky lightens almost immediately and the rain stops as if on cue.

Dripping leaves provide a shower for the squawking blue jays who are enjoying a bath in the lake in the yard. The sun splits the layers of black clouds and its pink rays engulf my scrubbed yard in a rosy glow.

I open the porch windows and the smell of wet earth and plants fills me with a feeling of renewal. The dust and cares of the day have been washed away. For these few moments, my world is clean and pure.

Summer 1980

THE FUTILITY ROOM

Ideas and plans featured in magazines can usually be adapted for use in any home. There's only one significant point that editors fail to mention: once the room is completed, admire it—but don't try to live in it.

Adjacent to my kitchen in an alcove set off by two deeply gouged doors, one leading to the backyard and the other to the garage, stands my utility room. In nine square feet I have managed a room which is a combination pantry, library, mud room, wine cellar, sports equipment storage center and bath.

Originally the refrigerator nestled in this space but with five of us clamoring for the bathroom, we decided to convert the space into a quarter-bath. It could never qualify for a half-bath in any real estate ad.

When I saw the plans in a magazine for utilizing space for an additional bath, I eagerly incorporated the ideas—bright colors, cabinets, a window and plants on the shelves—into my nine square feet. The finished room was perfect. Then my family started to use the utility room.

I tried hard. All summer I vacuumed the dirt and sand from the corners and wiped up water spilled from balloons that burst before they could be smuggled outside for water fights. Wet bathing suits were thrown out the back door to hang on the line. This room, my pride and joy, would stay neat and clean.

Fishing season marked the beginning of the end. At the conclusion of each of my husband's fishing expeditions a new surprise awaited me. Smelly bait in plastic bags in the sink was put back into the freezer. Slippery fluke and bass plunked there were flipped back at him to clean in the yard. A pile of slithering eels proved to be too much. In my rush to escape from them, I smacked into the back door and badly bruised my knee. I approached the sink cautiously for the rest of the summer.

Throughout the autumn footballs, basketballs and shoulder pads were removed and stored in the cellar each night only to reappear by afternoon the following day. Then winter came and I gave up the good fight.

The corner sink was handy for soaked mittens, socks or sneakers and snowballs piled high for deposit in the freezer. A corner toilet handled every emergency and doubled as a seat for changing wet boots and snowsuits. The wall cabinets held first aid supplies for bumps and cuts, the spices that won't fit in the kitchen cabinet, three water pistols and six mis-matched mittens.

Now that spring is here the floor is the largest storage area with five pairs of boots lined neatly in a row. Water dripping silently from them forms a slow moving stream headed across the tile floor toward the door. Dry shoes are heaped on top waiting for the kids to claim them after they slosh in the back door. In one corner is piled a ten pound sack of potatoes, five pounds of onions (half in and half out of the bag) and a torn five pound container of rock salt topped by twenty pounds of bird seed. The birds eat first each day.

In the opposite corner rests a carton of oranges sent by my brother who is vacationing in Florida. A half-finished gallon of Chianti mellows in another corner, a silent reminder of a week spent with three kids home for Christmas vacation—all of them sick.

This coldest corner of the house serves two purposes. It makes an excellent wine cellar, keeping the wine at a perfect serving temperature. And I no longer have to nag my children to hurry and get ready for school in the morning. No one lingers in this bathroom during cold weather.

The library is on the back of the toilet tank. A copy of "Meditations for Mothers", a Sports Illustrated from July, a booklet on "How to Pickle and Preserve", a Boy Scout handbook and three feet of rope used for practicing knots all rest there.

A pogo stick, a Christmas gift, leans against a wall decorated with my daughter's school art work. This hides the large cracks my husband has yet to fill. An excellent drying rack, the pogo stick has a ripped jacket and dirty hat on the handlebars and two pairs of dirty mittens dripping from each footrest.

Ready to shut the door so I won't have to look at the mess, I step back and open it wider instead. A thought has come to me: Where would all this clutter be if I didn't have my utility room?

March 1981

MY FIRST STAGE
PERFORMANCE

I was in the seventh grade when I made my theatrical debut—in front of Eddie Cook. I had a brief appearance as Mother Goose in third grade but as I remember had no lines to recite. This would be big-time. Our class was doing a take-off on the Arthur Godfrey radio show and I and two other girls would be singing two stanzas of the opening commercial for Campbell Soups: "Mmmm good—mmmm good—That's what Campbell Soups are mmmm good."

Eddie Cook would finally notice me. Not just notice me but really see me. He and the other eighth grade popular boys always sat in the front row in the middle of the auditorium during our school assemblies. I would be right on stage in front of him with a new black skirt and red sweater. He couldn't miss me.

After that I was sure I was bound to become part of his special group. I always seemed to be looking in from the fringe of the popular kids. They didn't ignore me yet they still didn't include me completely. Eddie and his crew always wanted me to play on their lunchtime or after-school baseball or football team. And they often sought advice when they wanted help in pursuing a girlfriend or when they needed help with their homework. But I wanted Eddie to chase me around the playground and tease me during lunch. That would show he really cared.

At last our big day came. Hands shaking, sick to my stomach and hoping words wouldn't stick in my throat, I stepped onto the stage with my two class-mates. Waiting for the radio announcer to introduce us, I checked to make sure Eddie was in the first row. He was—right in the middle. I glowed. "Mmmm good, mmmm good—that's what Campbell Soups are mmmm good." The three of us sang our hearts out.

Eddie was watching; he was even pointing at me. But he was laughing. He and his cohorts were rocking back and forth in their seats laughing. Laughing and pointing at us. He was supposed to be smiling at me not laughing at me. Face on fire, I wanted to disappear.

For days after that in the hallways, during gym class and on the way home from school Eddie and his friends never stopped teasing. "Hi Gerry. How's the soup? Mmmm good?" And they would roar with laughter. I laughed with them, dying inside.

A year later, after eighth grade graduation, I entered high school where Eddie was now a sophomore. Maybe I'd have another chance. The first time he saw me he started laughing and said, "Hi Ger, how's the soup?" I couldn't answer and hurried away so he wouldn't see my tears. I followed his wonderful blue eyes and blond hair through the grades hoping he would see me again but he never looked back.

10-01-02

QUIZZES

I love to take the personality quizzes that appear in many magazines such as: "Will you be a better cook for your second husband?" "How to discover the philosopher within you", "Creative Laziness"—things like that. I don't think I've ever completed one test using truthful answers, added up the points or true/false scores and have recognized the person described by the results.

Two of my recent attempts at discovering self were disasters. For "What Color Tells About You" I listed blue and red as co-favorites. Blue described someone reserved, calm and easy-going; red explained an extroverted, high-achieving perfectionist. No wonder my husband says he'll never know me. The second test was entitled "How Creative Are You?" Not very. I missed the lowest category—no talent but keep trying—and didn't even score enough points to qualify as a failure.

My latest challenge—"What Your Sleep Positions Tell About You" asks "Do you curl up like a cuddly kitten or stretch out like a leopard? Nocturnal postures reveal intimate secrets of your psyche!" The experts who developed this exam made definitive statements which left little room for argument. However, after reviewing their stated conclusions, I think my explanations make a lot more sense. For example: Fetal Position—"You would like nothing better than to return to the safety of the womb." Well, not quite. My flannel nightgown shrunk a lot in the dryer last time around and I'm curled up trying to keep neck and ankles covered and warm at the same time.

Prone Position—"Everything is under control. You're self-assured enough to turn your back on the world." Actually I fell on my face into bed exhausted after a wild day at work and company for dinner. I couldn't move if I wanted to. My husband has so many covers on the bed it's impossible to turn over.

On The Side of the Bed—"You have a difficult time asserting yourself." In fact, I've slept on this mattress with my husband for more than fifteen years and my body has molded the lumps and hollows on my side to perfection. My mattress and I unite each evening as smoothly as interlocking puzzle pieces.

Diagonally—"Lying fully across the bed on a diagonal demonstrates that you're a highly assertive individual." The joy is that my husband and brother are away for a weekend of fishing and the whole bed is mine for two nights.

Supine—"Sleeping on your back proves you are a very generous and giving individual, sympathetic to the needs of others." I don't know about that but the doctor said I had to sleep on my back to help a sciatica flare-up and I'm extremely sympathetic to my own needs.

One Foot Over The Edge—"Actually you don't like to sleep, even when you're exhausted. You're extremely active and energetic and involved in too many projects to allow much time for rest." Who are they kidding? I'm ready to run because an intestinal virus is flying through the family and I have to move fast when I hear "Ma come quick". After trips to the bathroom to offer assistance, two beds are stripped, remade and a load of sheets and towels thrown into the washer.

Sphinx—"In this position you're face down with your head resting on your arms and knees drawn up beneath your head so that your back is in the air like a beetle." This is simply a lesson on how to play dead on Sunday morning. After attending mass on Saturday night so I can steal a few extra hours of sleep, no one better come near me.

Sitting Up—"To put it simply, you sleep sitting up with your hands at your side because you have difficulty relaxing." Indeed, it's the height of hay fever season, neither the vaporizer nor prescriptions from the doctor have alleviated my misery and I'm merely trying to achieve a basic human function—breathing.

Arms and Legs Crossed—"Unconsciously you are telegraphing that you don't want to let others in, for you have a strong fear of being hurt." Well, I have a daughter terrified by a violent thunderstorm who has wiggled her way between me and my husband and unless I'd like to try and move him—impossible—and it's easier to lie on the edge of the bed with arms and legs crossed so I don't roll onto the floor.

Now you have some alternative choices to help you categorize your own sleep positions, The authors of this quiz also had one interesting final suggestion: "By the way, you probably aren't aware of the positions you sleep in, so ask a friend."

1978

BUDDIES

The sun bakes my back as I walk toward the lakefront, my ten year old daughter's hand in mine. My husband and two sons are out fishing for the day so Nancy and I will have this time to ourselves. Vacation allows me to make up to her for all the hours I had pushed her aside during a busy, hectic year.

"Hi Sheila." Nancy scampers off toward the tall teenager headed down the path, another guest in our cottage colony. For just a second I feel hurt and then grin. Who needs this time together for reassurance—Nancy or me? I settle myself on the blanket in the soft sand listening to her squeal with delight as she reaches the raft with Sheila and Amy who is also vacationing here. Nancy proudly jumps off the raft and swims back quickly "just like the big girls". I feel proud of her abilities and self-assurance.

Tired at last, she drops onto the blanket next to me proclaiming, "I want to be an athlete when I grow up, mommy." My daughter is seeking a lifestyle for herself, following her role models who still frolic jubilantly in the shimmering water. "Want to go for a walk Nan?" "Gee mom, I'm kind of tired right now." Her sideways glance and sheepish look amuse me. Trying not to hurt my feelings, she gives me a reassuring pat on the arm.

After a rest Nan and I plunge into the cold pond together for the first time. She's solicitous, making sure it's not too cold for me. "Oooooh mommy, I love you!" she squeals, giving me a giant bear hug and submerging me at the same time. I tire easily and see the disappointment on her face as I leave the water after only a short time to collapse onto the blanket. In a moment she sits beside me and rests her arm on my shoulder. As the sun warms us I can feel the water bubbles prickle my skin as they evaporate. Gulls soar overhead; crows surrounding the lake gossip noisily. I'm aware for the first time in endless months that I "feel" and this awareness brings the realization I'm coming alive again after the numbing winter with its responsibilities and frenetic pace.

Nancy soon disappears up the hill to get herself a snack from the cabin and I'm alone again, amused. She returns and shares her potato chips and iced tea with Sheila and Amy and then charges into the pond with them trying to match their proficient backstroke. I'm impressed with the loveliness of one and the athletic ability of the other. Both are bright, sharing girls who are now vacation friends. Their openness and honesty toward each other is refreshing as they compare notes about their abilities, school, parents and boys. Nancy's beaming face reveals her delight at being included. I watch my daughter as she frolics in the water; all inhibitions have dropped away. She sings, twirls and churns through the green coolness.

Finally she hauls herself up onto the raft, blue swimsuit glistening, tossing the water from her hair in imitation of her new friends. She's leaner, older, more independent. I picture my daughter in a few short years, a young lady maturing and growing away from me but somehow it doesn't bother me. I know she will be fine.

1984

THE OUTCASTS

We were the outcasts in the family my grampa Willie and me. But I didn't mind because I was his favorite and that's all that mattered. Every Sunday my family was compelled to have dinner with my father's parents and his four sisters and their families. I hated going because I didn't want to get dressed up and have my hair curled and was constantly admonished to keep my mouth shut. My brother was always the "good boy" who played politely with my dozen cousins and my mom kept after me because I disappeared with gramp all the time.

Although my grandparents were born in Sicily, aside from gramp and my father, this was the coldest, most withholding Italian family I ever knew. I think the passionate Italian blood in my grandmother's veins changed to seawater on her trip across the Atlantic and she passed it on to her daughters. When I was the first to become engaged and bring my fiancé—an extra person—to a holiday dinner, my aunt made sure I paid her $3 for the extra ravioli on his plate.

When we arrived each Sunday, my aunts and uncles sat as mannequins in the same stiff circle in the living room. My aunts' dour faces and solemn greetings reminded me of a wake and the only items missing were a casket and body in the center of the room. Straining, my uncles would occasionally laugh and tell a joke. They drank a lot of beer.

My aunts greeted me with polite disdain. Since my brother and I were the only cousins who didn't attend Catholic school, we were judged to be without any academic skills or redeeming social graces. I didn't know anything about First Fridays, novenas or how to talk to nuns. Mass once a week was enough for me.

Gramp made it a point never to be ready when company arrived, one of the ways he rebelled against his nagging wife and four daughters. I couldn't understand why he didn't talk back to them, but as I grew older I realized he had many subtle ways of not conforming to their wishes. He'd greet us at the front door in his undershirt, often marked with a large red stain, a sign he had enjoyed a nip of his homemade Chianti before we arrived.

His thick white hair stuck out in every direction and he always needed a shave. He would grab me roughly and rub his whiskers up and down my cheek while I protested wildly, loving every minute. His tiny blue eyes twinkled with the promise of a smooth sweet cheek to be kissed before the end of the day. Gramp was the only one in the family who ever hugged with love and gusto and when I was encircled in his arms I felt as if I was inside a big warm bubble.

My cousins routinely played their boring organized games and the adults continued the same repetitive conversation week after week. As soon as I could I ran to gramp to have some fun. He would be in the kitchen, flour up to his elbows with just enough accidentally sprinkled on the worn linoleum floor for someone else to clean up. A stiff white butcher apron which reached the floor was tied tightly around his potbelly. He had short legs, a stocky frame and by the time I was ten we were the same height.

Gramp rolled out the dough for the ravioli on a smooth porcelain tabletop using a meticulously cleaned long-handled broomstick—much to the annoyance of his wife and daughters. "They don't do the work, so they should keep quiet and let me do it my way," he grumbled. "This broom handle works better than anything I've ever used and spreads the dough smoothly."

After the dough was rolled and ravioli cut and filled with cheese, we disappeared, leaving the mess for my aunts to clean up. Often we hid in the garden behind the garage and out of sight of the house so gramp could sneak a cigar. Ruby colored grapes which covered the arbor formed a cool, fragrant arch. The damp black earth smelled good enough to eat. Eggplant, basil, zucchini and plum tomatoes sprawled together in a colorful jumble. This was gramp's domain and he chased anyone who tried to join us. Rough and grumbly, his voice scared my cousins but I knew the gentleness underneath and was never afraid.

On rainy days we went to his woodshop in the cellar—a magical place. The low ceiling, dirt floor and hazy light filtering through the tiny window transformed the room into a secure haven. A strong smell of woodchips and varnish filled the room. Gramp could create anything out of wood and I thought he was a genius. My most cherished possession is the bookcase I helped him build. But he abandoned attempts to teach me to whittle and carve when he realized all my fingers were thumbs. "Aw, you're only a girl—what good are you anyway?" he'd complain and then give me a bear hug.

Too often gramp disappeared and I knew where he was but wouldn't tell anyone when he was gone. He liked to visit his friends at the neighborhood bar around the corner. Gramp drank too much whiskey sometimes and I got upset when he went there and would try to get him to stay home. When he didn't, I had to go and get him before he had to face the squawking of his wife and daughters.

Once my cousins trailed after me around the corner and I approached the open door of the bar, my heart beating wildly. This was forbidden territory for my aunts had warned us about the awful people who went there. Peering into the smoky darkness, I saw gramp sitting on a stool sipping his whiskey and talking to the bartender. Shaking, I inched toward the creaky screen door looking behind me for my cousins' support. But they had run home, eager to tattle. I ran inside and clung to gramp's leg.

"Up you go little gal." And there I was on the stool, staring through the dim light, trying desperately to see all the terrible things that must surround me. Gramp bought me a cherry Coke and I wanted to stay but saw his watery eyes and knew we had to go. "Come on gramp, let's go home before everybody gets riled up again." "Bahh, can't a man have a drink in peace away from all those women and kids?"

"Come on gramp, let's go." I was getting scared. He usually listened to me and if I didn't bring him home right away mom would be after me since I wasn't supposed to leave the house. "Oh well, might as well make the ladies happy," he laughed as he slid unsteadily off the stool. I put my arm through his and guided him home.

We had a plan when we were late. I stayed in the garden while he collected lettuce, tomatoes, peppers and basil to take in for the salad. "Was in the garden the whole time," he insisted to my aunts. "Stop complaining, I was snoozing."

Finally the family sat down to eat—my cousins neat, clean and polite, my mother glaring at my dirty dress and uncombed hair. I wanted to sit next to gramp but there was a seating order according to family rank and I don't think God himself could have changed it. Gramp magically re-appeared clean shaven, his hair plastered flat against his head with Jeris' Brilliantine. Eyes refreshed by splashes of cold water now sparkled, reflecting the deep blue of his one Sunday dress shirt. I never could figure out how he managed this transformation so quickly.

After we finished dinner the adults stayed to talk and nibble on fruits, nuts and pastries. Too busy arguing or complaining, they didn't see me slide off my chair, sneak down to gramp's end of the table and, if I was lucky, manage to slip beneath the floor-length tablecloth. I'd nudge gramp's knee and piece by piece he would hand me the orange slices which had soaked up the Chianti in the pitcher on the table. The bitter taste took my breath away but the treat was special because only I shared it with him.

When it was time to leave I had to kiss my aunts and uncles goodbye as they stood stiffly and I resented this meaningless gesture. Then I got to gramp. The cheek he rubbed against mine as he squeezed me was baby soft, the sweet smell of powder and cologne enveloped him. I never wanted to leave. "See you next Sunday, babe." That's all I wanted to hear.

SURPRISE VISITOR

My indulgence in self-pity had kept me awake half the night and finally pushed me out of bed much earlier than usual. It was still dark and I muttered and grumbled about the unfairness of life as I poked downstairs and made my way into my small cluttered kitchen. I didn't need to turn on the light to know my family had left a pile of snack dishes in the sink and crumbs and papers scattered over the counter.

As I curled my toes up away from the icy kitchen floor, I stumbled over a chair and banged my knee. Good start for the day. I put on the teakettle, planning to enjoy some extra time without the usual mad rush to work. I slumped onto the chair and dropped two slices of bread into the toaster. Peace. I could gather my wits and try to shake off the blue mood which had pursued me for days. Suddenly there was a rustling sound behind me. Please—not one of the kids already; it was too early. I needed time to think.

Before I could turn around, something brushed against my arm. A helium-filled "Happy Birthday" balloon, which had spent the night on the middle of the living room ceiling, bobbed slowly overhead into the kitchen. It was the lone survivor of a cluster of balloons we had brought home from an 80th birthday party for a favorite uncle the night before.

I looked up and realized the force of hot air from the heat vents must have sent the sphere on its travels toward the kitchen after I had clicked on the heat. It floated slowly around the kitchen, swaying gently back and forth over the table. Its bright foil face was covered with myriad yellow starbursts, blue rockets and a border of red stars. The bold "Happy Birthday" emblazoned across its face curved into a big grin that seemed to smile down on me.

I chuckled as the balloon bobbed against my shoulder, poking me as I ate my toast. Gently, I pushed it away from me and it floated to the other side of the room. I watched fascinated as it circled slowly in the current of hot air pumping out of the heat vent, first swinging over the stove, then bumping off the refrigerator—but still intent on making its way back to me.

At last it settled by my side. It nudged me and then backed off slightly, nudged and sidled back again. My laughter broke the silence as I looked up and saw its benevolent grin saying, "Come on, it isn't that bad; life is good. Smile. It's gonna be a fine day".

I sat back in the chair and thought about my problems. Maybe they weren't that serious. It had been hectic for the past few months and I had somehow lost perspective along the way. My smiling visitor reminded me that a smile and sense of humor are two of the strongest allies I have to reach for before starting each day.

That was a week ago. As I write this in my upstairs bedroom my birthday visitor has floated up to provide encouragement. It's still visiting around my home, nudging my family with a gentle reminder that life is good if we take time to enjoy it.

ONCE UPON A SUMMER

I remember when it seemed only movie stars had swimming pools and there were no beach clubs or municipal pools. When we wanted to cool off, we ran through the sprinkler or attached the hose to the top of a stepladder, marveling at the rainbow as the sun shone through the spray.

Families owned one car and dad took it to work every day. Mom could stay home and relax because kids couldn't ask, "Where are we going today?" They just played in their own neighborhood. Mothers didn't have to work to make ends meet and kids didn't need summer camp. No one had much money but no one seemed to mind either. We didn't know we were missing any fun.

There were no summer sport leagues. The kids on the block got together after supper, played stickball in the street or marched around the corner to the school playground to play kickball or softball. No TV, video games or mopeds, but kick-the-can, hide-and-seek, tag and SPUD.

No one went to summer school for enrichment or make-up work. And somehow, we all learned, passed on to the next grade and managed to cope with growing up. When we were bored, we were expected to entertain ourselves and mom could say, "Get lost", without feeling guilty.

A bike trip to the park was a big deal. Not on a ten-speed but on a Schwinn with balloon tires that made the ride an endurance test. The bike was safe, the lake clean and the fish living there grew larger every year.

Our homes didn't have air conditioning so we all sat outside every night to cool off with some homemade lemonade and watched the stars and fireflies brighten our evening. Hot dogs, well-done over a homemade charcoal grill and a glass of root beer shared with friends under the grape arbor was a fancy barbecue.

We seemed to have more friends than neighbors. There were few fences but lots of holes in hedges to cut through to the next yard. When it was too hot to move, I would lie on the porch glider, watching the clouds and dream secret dreams. Or watch a spider spin his web and marvel at the scurrying ants carrying food to their families in the anthill, one crumb at a time.

We didn't have to work at enjoying summer—we just did.

SPLIT SCREEN

Through the porch window I see my neighbors, an elderly couple, sitting in their backyard enjoying the beautiful autumn day. Relaxed in faded weathered beach chairs, they face each other as they talk. A pink sweater covers her shoulders; the cat snoozes curled in the pocket of her lap. He wears a Yankee baseball cap and takes slow deliberate puffs on his pipe. As she speaks she learns forward, bobbing and shaking her head emphatically to emphasize her viewpoint. Her smile and soft laughter brighten the warm afternoon.

Expressive hands punctuate his conversation as he pokes and waves his pipe in the air, punching holes in her arguments. They are in their eighties, truly lovers. It amazes me they have this much to share after more than fifty years of marriage. Although he's been retired for many years, it's exciting to see them find such joy in each other.

Between our two yards a clothesline crowded with toddlers' bright overalls and play clothes flies in the brisk wind. A young couple and their two children live next door and I feel a kinship with them as I watch them raise their children and deal with problems I've already faced. The young mother opens her back door and walks across the lawn to visit her neighbors. She is one of a vanishing breed—a mother who enjoys being home with her children and experiencing the joys, surprises and frustrations of their daily escapades.

Her three year old son races across the grass, a lollipop clutched in his fist. He suddenly veers to the left and charges toward the birdbath. Stopping short, he peeks over his shoulder at his mom and then tosses the lollipop into the water. His baby sister bounds forward unsteadily trying to catch up with him. The bright calico sunbonnet she wears to protect her ears from the cool breeze frames a cherub face split by the same wide grin her mother wears daily.

Suddenly I'm aware that I'm midway in life between these two sets of neighbors who are sharing the lovely afternoon and realize I'm content where I am. My three children are almost grown, yet they still need the nurturing and loving environment their dad and I try to provide. They're old enough to allow us more free time to reach and discover new paths to explore together.

I don't envy this mom the job of raising a family. I wish I could have had the knowledge as I raised toddlers that I possess today. There would have been fewer mistakes, fewer heartaches. But somehow my children survive because of and in spite of me. It's not an easy world in which to raise children and I'm thankful we've come this far with out family still intact. Our growing process never stops.

Acutely aware of my aging lately, I dislike the new wrinkles and age spots which multiply steadily. My vanity surprises me for I expected to grow old gracefully. But at times I find myself resenting and fighting this inevitable process. Many loved ones have died within the past few years and I'm sometimes preoccupied with thoughts of my own mortality. But I have confidence and faith that acceptance will come.

There is peace and beauty in the picture framed by my window. My friend and her children are a reminder of my past and I'm thankful that shared joys and tears have imbued me with an increased inner strength. I see in the venerable couple before me the beauty and promise of what my life can be.

1982

BACK-TO-SCHOOL NIGHT

Mothers occasionally seen with coats thrown over bathrobes are glamorous in bright dresses. Fathers have traded work clothes for collar and tie. Eager teachers happily welcome this new group of parents. Moms are smiling, dads enduring—it's back to school night.

Smooth and shiny, the hallway floors smell of newly applied wax. The fresh yellow paint on the foyer walls covers the repulsive green color which depressed everyone for years. Hall showcases are lit to show off pumpkins, witches and ghosts peeping over fences.

"Citizen of the Month", "Most Improved Citizen". Two large posters hang on either side of the school's front door, the focal point in the main hallway. A child is nominated from each class and the proud winners receive certificates at a monthly assembly program. The list does not include the names of the scholars or athletes. These are the names of kids who don't usually achieve recognition or win awards. The principal and his staff have stated their main goal is to improve the self-image of each child and this is one way of achieving their objective.

Hats too large rest on the eyebrows of Cub Scouts struggling as they enter the auditorium trying to reach the stage with heavy flags for opening exercises. The principal speaks first, encouraging parents to call him with problems or suggestions. He stresses that the only way to maintain good home-school dialogue is to keep in touch. The PTA president rushes through her portion of the meeting as she knows parents are anxious to hear the Superintendent of Schools. He reviews past accomplishments and outlines goals for the new school year. The hearty applause reflects the impression he has made on parents.

The audience stirs restlessly as the smell of brewing coffee wafts up from the cafeteria below. They are anxious to get to the classrooms. Parents who waited in the hallway for the business meeting to conclude grow louder. Too disinterested to participate, they will be the first to complain that "nobody told us" when a new school policy is initiated.

I'm delighted to find my daughter's fifth grade classroom bright and airy. Books are everywhere. Brain teaser games are stacked on a table, puzzles and resource materials piled high next to them. Challenges are in every corner. Bright maps and charts re-acquaint us with the rest of the world. A model of the solar system is strung on wire with a bright yellow sun in one corner and vividly colored planets positioned in order along the wire to the opposite side of the room. Fifth grade is more challenging than the confusing fractions and dull history texts I remember. Flipping to the table of contents in my daughter's reading book, I am greeted by a list that includes Greek and Indian myths, Yeats, Longfellow and Tolstoy. A slight change from Dick and Jane.

"I expect the best from your children and won't settle for less," the teacher says. "I haven't looked at their previous records and will judge them by the work they do for me." A bright and interesting woman, the classroom reflects her personality. "The children have been asked to write a composition—'Why I Like Me' to tie in with our self-image goal. Some of them may not bring this assignment home to you. I've told them it's up to them if they want to share it with you." She smiles gently, for she knows some parents do not readily accept this idea.

Bright orange cards are passed out and the room buzzes—the new fifth grade report cards with numbered grades eliminated. Marks now range from "little progress" to "outstanding progress". "All academic and social areas are checked where improvement is needed," explains the teacher. "You know exactly where your child stands measured against himself. Please try to resist measuring him against others." Some parents are quite vocal in commending the teacher for her endorsement of the card while the polite frowns of others as they exit the room leave little doubt about their feelings.

Resisting the aroma of coffee, I dash home to finish some chores. After the stuffy classroom the damp night air feels refreshing. I am happy. My daughter is being taught by a teacher who cares.

October 1984

SOMETHING IS WRONG

I read an article the other day which paraphrased text from the Book of Deuteronomy that referred to nations acting as a "model of neighborliness". The basic premise was "a society that cannot be generous to those in need will not be blessed". An optimist, it takes a lot to make me feel distressed or upset. But in recent months, the direction my country seems to be taking leaves me feeling extremely pessimistic.

When I view the art exhibits and enjoy the wonderful variety of concerts available on Cape Cod I despair. Where will we find our future artists and musicians if music and art are the first items in the school curriculum to be discarded as budgets are cut in schools across the country? Classes grow larger and unmanageable in many schools as teachers are laid off due to financial constraints. Some school districts are shortening the school day and there is discussion about shortening the school year.

Pre-school and after-school programs for children of working parents, often single mothers, are cancelled. Where do these children go as their parents struggle, many working two jobs, to feed their families? America Corps, a program which enabled thousands of college students to earn money toward school tuition by working in a variety of social-service positions where they helped children, is being cut drastically.

Many middle class families can no longer hold onto the American dream of home ownership. The number of homeless and families without any medical coverage grows by the day. Low-cost and affordable housing are dirty words in many communities. Unemployed bread-winners are no longer able to pay their mortgages and the number of foreclosures is rising.

There are too many upsetting circumstances in our society today for me to list. But there is one more. Veterans. Memorial Day and the 4th of July are always important holidays to me. I feel a tremendous sense of pride every Memorial Day at a parade or commemorative ceremony. I watch the evening concert on television from Washington, DC and view the faces of veterans, generations of men and women in the audience who have risked their lives so that I can be free and enjoy the life I have. I whisper a silent thank you to each of them.

This year millions of dollars in aid for veterans was cut from the federal budget, leaving many without medical benefits or prescriptions. Veteran's organizations claim there is now an $15 billion shortfall. These men and women are our heroes. How do they take care of themselves now? The federal budget is already running at a $250 billion deficit, partially due to September 11th and the cost of the war in Iraq.

We send young men and women into war to help keep us free and safe. We send millions of dollars to foreign countries through various forms of aid. Yet there isn't enough money to take care of our veterans and others in our society desperately in need. Something is very wrong.

September 2003

HALLOWEEN

I was about eleven when Judy, Janie and I went out for Mischief Night for the first time. That was the night before Halloween when kids would go out for fun such as soaping car windows, ringing doorbells and running away, upsetting garbage cans on the front lawn, etc. Just a little fooling around. We thought it was a big deal because our parents let us go out with the promise we wouldn't do any damage or bother anyone. We didn't really know what to do to "make mischief" but felt so important to be out with the big kids. Actually I was kind of scared because they teased and tried to frighten us when they passed us on the street. I wanted to go home but couldn't tell my friends because they would think I was a sissy.

After wandering around bored and scared for awhile, we figured out how to rig up a plastic pumpkin on a stick and set a flashlight in it. Then we would hold the lighted pumpkin up to the window of a neighbor's home, tap on the window, yell and then run away. We thought hiding in the bushes and watching neighbors come to the window was great fun and never thought of ourselves as peeping toms. We just giggled our way through the neighborhood.

Then we got to Mrs. Schilling who was a widow. Her husband had been a nice man who always smiled and talked to us and never made us move when we were playing stickball in the street by his driveway. But Mrs. Schilling was a grouchy lady who never smiled and chased us away from the front of her house—which was the best location on the block for running bases. She made our lives miserable.

There was a light in her front window so we got the pumpkin ready to scare her. We'd show her for sure. Tap, tap, tap on the window but no response. After trying this a few times, Jane went to the front door and rang the doorbell as we tapped on the window again. We'd really annoy her; she wouldn't know which way to turn.

And then she opened the front door quicker than I ever thought she could move and grabbed Janie by the coat collar. Mrs. Schilling was crying. "Darn, darn, darn you kids. You scared the heart out of me. I was reading the paper, heard a noise, looked up and there was that awful pumpkin staring at me. My glasses fell off when I jumped out of the chair. A poor old lady like me. You kids are cruel; why don't you leave me alone?" She continued to cry, still holding Janie by the collar.

We wanted to run away but couldn't leave Janie stranded. Silent, the three of us stared at Mrs. Schilling. "Well," she said. "Do you realize how much you scared me? How would you feel if someone did that to your parents? Now get out of here and go home." She pushed Janie away and slammed the door. No one would admit it but I think we all felt sorry for her. Being out for Mischief Night didn't seem to be much fun any more so we returned quietly to our homes.

About a week later we were playing stickball when a shrieking ambulance came roaring up the street and stopped in front of Mrs. Schilling's house. The medics ran inside and were in there a long time. We sat silently on her lawn as anxious neighbors gathered. I was afraid to think.

The medics brought her out on a stretcher and she looked terrible—gray and wrinkled and sick. We heard the next day that she had a severe heart attack and died shortly after reaching the hospital. I felt terrible. I never said anything to my friends but I wonder if they had the same thought: we had scared her to death. Until I married and moved out of the neighborhood, every time I walked by her house I felt the same guilt.

THE EAGLE

I glanced out the window and noticed my two sons had interrupted their football game and were standing in the street in front of the house, mouths agape, staring toward the back yard. "Mom, come quick, there's an eagle at the top of the tree." Probably one of the large crows that visit us often was looking for supper. I rushed out into the icy air and turned and saw, perched proudly at the top of the tallest oak in our yard, an American Bald Eagle.

The fact that he was surrounded by houses, the congestion from two nearby strip malls and the roar of rush hour traffic from the Parkway only a few minutes away didn't seem to faze him. "We heard a loud whoosh and slapping sound. When we looked up there he was tearing at a squirrel's nest near the top of the tree."

Afraid we might scare him off if we ran into the yard, we rushed into the house and stood staring at him through the sunroom windows. About three feet tall with a massive chest of white feathers flecked with brown, he had glittering yellow eyes that stared straight ahead. The squirrels that fled had leaped to the bottom of the tree and, frozen in fear, were pressed spread-eagled against the rough bark.

Proud and aloof, the eagle surveyed his surroundings, his talons gripping the highest branch. He sat motionless, his powerful beak clamped shut as the wind ruffled the white feathers around his neck. I was afraid of him. Perhaps aware we were watching him, he swooped away a few minutes later, landing in a tree about fifty yards from us in the cemetery which abuts our back yard. Even with binoculars it was extremely difficult to pick him out since he blended in perfectly with the stark tree branches surrounding him. When we did get a good look at him, we saw his golden eyes staring at us, annoyed, not willing to come closer. For ten minutes he sat perched in the tree observing the squirrel's nest.

Amazed and fascinated that this majestic bird should visit my yard, I recalled vivid scenes from a recent National Geographic television special I had seen about eagles and California condors, the mightiest of birds. By appearing on the scene the eagle stretched my imagination and I could picture him soaring between mountain peaks, searching for dinner for his family. For these moments it seemed as if we were part of his natural habitat. He appeared completely oblivious of the fact he was the outsider, not us.

At last he noticed the darkening sky and decided to look elsewhere for dinner. With a final circle over our heads, he dipped his wings in farewell and soared away.

This morning the blue jays and cardinals battle at the bird feeder and the squirrels are busy repairing their battered nest. My eyes search the sky with the hope that my regal visitor will return, a proud, free silhouette etched against the red-streaked sky.

12-15-83

THE FIG TREE

I yanked and tore at the large weed which would not let go of its hold in the earth. Finally I got it half way out, but it was so stubborn I was exhausted from the struggle and quit trying. My father had died two weeks earlier. It was the first week of November and I was clearing out his beloved backyard garden. I thought of leaving the dead plants and unharvested rotting vegetables until spring but ached each time I saw the wasted plants. My mom must have felt the same because she asked if I could find time to clean up the garden. She couldn't bear the constant reminder of dad each time she looked out her kitchen window.

"Oh Lord, what happened to daddy's fig tree? It looks as if the frost has heaved it out of the ground." Mom had come out of the house to check on my progress. She gently touched the "weed" I had been struggling to pull out a few minutes earlier. A sick feeling in my stomach pushed into my throat as I knelt beside the plant. I hadn't known. It looked like a weed. Dad's friend had given it to him two years ago. My father had nursed it and checked its progress daily because he wanted a fig tree the same as his father had when dad was a boy growing up. It had grown only a few inches but had produced some leaves with the promise of more growth. "Wait till next year," he would laugh when we teased him about it.

"The kids were probably digging out here, Mom," I choked. Never could I tell her how I had struggled to pull it out. The dirt around it was loose, so I patted it back around the exposed roots. "We'll see how it is in the spring." I took mom inside for a cup of tea. Sick and guilty, I couldn't continue my work.

I never finished the garden that fall. Through the winter, every time I visited mom my eyes were drawn to that solitary stick in the middle of the garden. Unspoken guilt and shame engulfed me. I knew it was dead.

In May, I returned to the garden which was now overrun with weeds. At least they hid the tree from view. Mom had sold her home and was moving in another month. I couldn't leave the mess for the new owners. Dad would want his plot to look neat and well kept.

Furiously, I ripped and tugged at the strong, healthy weeds. Although the sun shone brightly, I felt as cold as stone. I was saying goodbye to my dad, my yard, my childhood. I reached to pull out the last row of brush and stopped. In front of me stood the fig tree. The tiny stick was covered with leaves and new shoots reached up from the ground.

Tears rolled down my cheeks as I stroked the leaves. One word sprang into my mind—resurrection. Dad was here with me in his garden. God had given new life to this stick I had yanked from the ground and left for dead last winter. The core of bitterness inside me slowly dissolved and was replaced by a warm feeling of acceptance and hope.

I dug out the tree and carefully wrapped it in burlap to transplant it into my garden. That was almost thirty years ago. Today I picked the first fig of the season and knew dad was with me as I savored the sweetness of the fruit.

May 1976

GETTING CONNECTED

✦

(Husband-wife conversation already censored)

I'm going to clean the bottom of the shower. You mean the floor? No. I mean the bottom of the shower. Well the bottom of the shower is the floor. No, it's not the floor; it's the bottom of the shower. The floor is clean. Is it where you stand when you take a shower? Yes. Well then it's the floor. It's not the floor; the floor is outside the shower where the sink and toilet rest. Good—go and clean the floor on the bottom of the shower.

Please get the butter out of the refrigerator and put it on the dish. There's no butter in here. There are two sticks in the box on the door. You mean in the freezer. No, on the refrigerator door—two sticks in the box. But I keep the butter in the freezer, so that's where it is. I know but I got a box out of the freezer because we needed to melt some when we had steamed clams. Why didn't you tell me you moved it? What's the difference, there's another box in the freezer and we needed the butter. But you didn't let me know. You were busy steaming the clams and drinking beer, why should I tell you about butter then, who cares if I take a box. I care. I like to keep track of things for the shopping list. Please get out a stick of butter from the refrigerator door and put it on the dish. You mean from the freezer??????

Running electrical wire from the basement to the first floor to provide a new outlet to hook up a ceiling fan by "snaking" the wire up through a wall. Now when you see the wire move, start to pull on it, gently so it doesn't get lost in the wall. Ok. Do you understand what I mean? Pull the wire gently so it doesn't get lost in the wall. Right. Do you see it? No. Do you see it now? No. Now? No. Why not. I don't know, but there's no wire up this far yet. Why not? How am I supposed to know; you're doing this job, I just help out. You call this helping? Don't get smart. All right I'll come up and check. There's no wire here. That's what I told you.

Ok, now do you see it. Yes, just a little but I can't grab it yet. Why not? Because it's not up far enough to grab. Well stick your finger in the hole and see if you can reach it. I can't reach it; the opening isn't big enough. Try harder to get your finger in and pull it up. I'm not going to slice my hand on this rough cut in the plaster you made. Ok, it should be through now. Ok, I see it. Pull. I am. Pull harder. I am. What's wrong? It won't budge. Which way are you pulling? Up. What the hell does that mean, up?

Up means up. Does that mean up toward you, up in the air or up and away from you? What? Are you pulling it straight up or toward you? Toward me. No, no, pull it straight up toward the ceiling. How am I supposed to know that. Because that's what up means, up straight, not up toward you. Since when. Gerry...................

Food shopping. Lemons are fifty cents each. I know. How much is the bag of lemons. I don't know. Don't you care? No; if we need lemons, we need lemons, right? Don't you care about prices? Yes, but we need lemons. I use them for clams and for ice tea. I know; we need lemons. Well, pick out a couple. No, not those two, they're not a good color. They're yellow. But not a bright yellow. Do you want to pick them out? No, you can. Ok, here. They're too big, get smaller ones, they're better.

7-5-03

GREEN AND GOLD

I wander out into the backyard determined to collect a few bright flowers to bring inside to cheer me up. A fresh wind promises to clear away the soggy air we've battled for weeks. Clouds of mosquitoes revive in the breeze and escort me across the lawn. I feel old, unappreciated and discouraged. Previously I wrote a column entitled "On the Bright Side" but my son complains lately he hasn't found much of my writing to be cheery. I don't want to admit to him or myself that as I grow older sometimes it seems difficult to find a bright spot in each day. But I still know there's a good side to almost every bad situation if we look hard enough.

The holly tree a friend gave me rests in a pot waiting to be planted but looks as if it has breathed its last as I brush the few remaining brown leaves from its stem. My clematis had started life as a lush green vine full of buds which are now shriveled and dropping to the ground. Meanwhile, my neighbor's sister plant is top-heavy with deep purple blossoms. She throws three or four different flowering plants into a wooden planter in the spring, goes off for the summer and returns home in the fall to a cascade of colorful blossoms. It's not fair. Two pots of white petunias rest on the iron plant stand. Bought only a few days ago, they've succumbed to a winged invader's digestive system.

It seems a blight has settled in my yard. Hostas that line the back fence provide a home to what I thought was mildew but turned out to be zillions of white hopping creatures which make my skin itchy. The oak and apple tree leaves resemble ragged lace. Caterpillar or moth—which one devours? I think they both do. Black-Eyed Susans planted in my proposed "English Country Garden" have been reduced to ugly rotting stems. Apparently the fungus in the soil we tried to kill last year is still reproducing happily. I tie up the gladiolus, yank a few weeds and decide this jumbled mess is not worth the effort.

I round the corner of the house and stop short. It's green and gold time, my favorite time of day. The few quiet minutes before sunset when the sun hangs suspended, its rays slanting through the trees and bushes, transforming my yard into a fresh oasis of shimmering copper hues. This is my time. Time to stop, take a few deep breaths and regroup for a new day.

The freshly watered pink impatiens in the corner shimmer and sparkle after their shower. Blue masses of hydragenia dance in the ever-freshening breeze. The lawn, which has been fighting for survival, has revived. More birds have returned this summer and chatter a goodnight chorus. Too quickly the sun sets and I head into the house to clean up the table and dishes, not really surprised once again an ever-present bright spot has rounded out my day.

1984

<u>KEVIN</u>

Nancy hesitated as we walked up the broad steps into our church. "What's the matter, mommy, you look sad." I smiled down at my seven year old, not surprised she sensed my mood since she was an intuitive and sensitive child. "Oh, nothing, honey. I just feel a little nervous for Kevin." I felt a sick lump in my stomach and wished this night was over. Christopher, thirteen, and my husband Roger had already found seats for us in one of the first pews in the church so we would be able to see Kevin clearly.

Parishioners quickly filled the seats, eager to participate in the Lenten Holy Thursday services. Members of the senior Catholic Youth Organization (CYO) would each read a passage from the Bible, one for each station of the cross in remembrance of Christ's suffering. Kevin's reading was for the Twelfth Station of the Cross—Christ dies. Socially immature and with few friends, he had at last found a small niche within the CYO group which was led by an understanding and compassionate priest. Kev had been thrilled to invite many family friends and neighbors to join us for the service.

I was proud but upset that Kevin had volunteered. His childhood had been filled with emotional pain. A chronic asthmatic, he also experienced serious learning disabilities which made each day of school a trial for him. Awkward and with poor coordination, he was considered a klutz by peers who didn't include him in sports activities or games. Labeled "retard" by classmates, he was a severe stutterer. Now fifteen and a junior in high school he saw a speech therapist weekly at school since his speech still became unintelligible when he was nervous or upset.

But Kevin also possessed a joy and zest for life I envied. His wonderful optimism helped him cope and compensate for problems he faced daily. We had adopted Kevin and brought him home when he was only a week old. Roger and I loved him like crazy and helped him in every way we could. But neither of us possessed Kevin's inherent accepting and non-judgmental personality. He considered everyone he met a friend. Through the years I often wished I could meet his birth parents to discover which of them (or perhaps both) enjoyed the joyous spirit they had passed on to our child.

The buzz of conversation quieted as Monsignor walked to the podium and greeted us warmly. He spoke softly, gently reminding us of what Christ had endured for us. All lights in the church clicked off with only the light over the lectern glowing on the Bible. One by one the CYO members, dressed in simple white robes, solemnly shared their readings. Some were nervous and read so quickly it was hard to understand them while others, composed and confident, read slowly and deliberately. Finally it was Kevin's turn.

He smiled as he opened the Bible to the passage he had practiced reading endlessly at home the last few weeks. My husband's hand closed over mine. Chris and Nancy looked at me for reassurance I was unable to provide. "The…..the….the…..", Kevin began. He stopped. His mouth twisted slowly as he tried painfully to say the next word. Nothing. We sat paralyzed in the quiet stillness. He wasn't stuttering; he was "blocked", unable to speak.

I looked away from him and tried not to cry. My family stared straight ahead. None of us could look at each other. Then, as we all waited in the soundless black church, I slowly felt a tiny warm glow flicker inside of me. It grew slowly until I felt consumed by its radiance. Moments later, I realized it had to be the prayers of everyone in the church forming a slow, single wave of hope directed toward Kevin, willing him to speak.

"Lord spoke." Two more words. Again his mouth contorted painfully but at last he continued his reading, halting for endless minutes between many words. He took a deep breath, a breath from which he seemed to draw strength from parishioners, family and friends. A smile crept into his eyes and over his face as he slowly and deliberately continued reading the exceptionally long passage. Finally he finished and stood there a moment. Unabashedly, he grinned broadly, gave a slight wave and stepped down from the lectern.

Nancy gave me a big hug and I had to grab Chris' hands to stop him from applauding. There were two more passages to be read. As the church lights clicked on one by one it seemed as if I had been on a long journey and was now returning to reality. My family sat silently a long time, each saying thank you in his own way before we went into the church hall to share refreshments with our church community.

I thought I might find Kevin upset or embarrassed but should have known better. God's wonderful gifts of optimism and joy hadn't let him down. He stood in the center of a large group, grinning broadly. "That was great, Kev. We all felt Jesus' pain when you were trying to speak." "Congratulations on a great job. You really hung in there. I would have flipped out." "Did you feel our prayers as we struggled with you?" "You really have guts". He laughed as more CYO members gathered around him, gently joshing and teasing. He was part of a group.

Father Charles, the CYO moderator, hugged Kevin tightly. "Well, Kevin. You are our hero tonight. I'm so proud of you. Every person here certainly could imagine the physical agony and mental suffering of Jesus when He hung on the cross as we watched you struggle. Your pain certainly showed how the Lord suffered before he died. You gave the word courage new meaning."

After the group drifted away, Kevin joined us for cake and punch. "Hey, mom. I told you not to worry. I knew I could do it. At first I really got upset when I got stuck. But then I remembered what my speech therapist tells me every week. She says, "Kev, when you have something to say and people care about you, they'll wait till you can finish. And isn't it great. She was right."

Spring 1981

THE LAST DAY

On this last day of vacation I wanted to spend time at one of my favorite spots—Mill Pond in Brewster. My two teenage sons protested vehemently. One envisioned a final day of stalking females, the other, roused from sleep under great protest proclaimed he wanted to soak up the sun and listen to music. City boys—not attuned to "bugs and all that nature stuff you like, Ma". But, good mother that I am, I insisted we spend the day as a family. Only Nancy, ten, was happy. A spider spinning a web fascinates her, too.

Once there the kids disappeared. My husband and I walked past the mill and the atmosphere immediately changed the tempo of our day. Shifting light and shadow, birds calling to each other, fish splashing to the surface in search of a fat bug—we had entered another world.

My husband started talking to a young teen from Minnesota vacationing with his family who had exceptional knowledge of fresh and salt water fishing techniques. I felt sorry for Rod as the boy bragged about the huge number of stripers and blues he had landed in Cape Cod Bay. After many years of trying, Rod is still trying to reel in his first "keeper" striped bass.

I inhaled my surroundings as I sat on the stone wall. Pale sunshine filtered through cobwebs, spotlighting captive insects, twisted leaves and a few gull feathers caught in a spider's trap. Lily pads bursting with delicate white flowers swayed gently in the water. Tangled vines hung from branches around me and provided a refuge where I felt totally alone.

Schools of small herring circled the pond as if on a merry-go-round. Their parents seemed to be herding the youngsters and reminded me of cowboys rounding up cattle. They forced their youngsters over the spillway to start on a downstream trip back to the sea until they are grown and ready to return to this refuge to spawn.

A catfish and his sister—prehistoric looking fish with evil eyes, whiskers and a nasty look—surfaced to trap some herring in the weeds and snatch them up for lunch. A water bug, his body set high on long legs, skimmed the surface of the pond, imagining himself a hydrofoil. Beetles skittered in circles like a child's wind-up toy. Next to me a spotted bug splashed down on to the surface, a seaplane making an abrupt landing. Bass, sunnies, pickerel and perch swam in harmony. Two eels oozed from beneath a patch of weeds, gliding toward the opposite bank. My skin prickled when I saw a water snake slither across the mirrored surface.

"Hey look," Chris yelled. "There's a big frog right by the bridge." Kevin raced to join him and I chuckled as I watched my two nature-haters trying to catch the large bullfrog. My meticulous husband, clad in white shorts and pink shirt plopped down on the grass, reached into the water, grabbed the frog and yelled, "Quick, get the camera. This is the first marine life I've landed in two weeks!" The frog rested on the grass a few moments, gave us a long disgusted look and took a giant leap back into the water.

Chris captured a large turtle which was sunning himself on a rock. Apparently used to intruders, the turtle showed no fear and blinked at us complacently. The kids wanted to take him back to our cottage but I suggested we leave him with his family. In a few moments a larger turtle, probably dad, paddled gently on the surface, followed by three offspring. "Look at this little one," squealed Nancy, pointing to the tiniest member of the group which slid off the bank and swam to catch up. My trio stared at me, apparently impressed with my knowledge of turtle family habits.

Too quickly, it was time to leave. We had been here only a few short hours and experienced just a tiny sample of the wonders of this pond community. I imagined the joy of being able to spend a year here. To experience the changing seasons, to hear the hums and cries, to smell, to feel the new rhythm of each day. To be.

8-27-85

PEANUT BUTTER AND JELLY

I approached the casket and hesitated. Dear God, don't let me laugh. All I could think of when I saw Aunt Ruthie was peanut butter and jelly. But the woman in the coffin couldn't be Ruthie. The face was a gray mask which belonged to someone else. Fake hands, lines of pewter wax clasping rosary beads. A stranger whose blonde hair was neatly styled.

My dad had four sisters and Ruthie was my favorite. As I sat down with the other mourners, I could hear her laughter and pictured her big toothy grin and sparkling eyes as she twirled around her summer home, dancing with my uncle Herman like a schoolgirl. Frayed nightgown swaying gently beneath a battered bathrobe, strands of dyed blonde, up-swept hair dangling down her neck and cheek as she kept time to the music, cigarette held at a Marlene Dietrich tilt—Ruthie was a presence.

From the time I was four until high school graduation, my mom, dad, brother and I spent two weeks every summer with Ruth, Herman and my three cousins at their seashore home. Mom found our vacations hurtful and difficult. Dad loved the beach but mom complained she always wanted to do something different. She criticized Ruthie's housekeeping and that she never worried about important things. I couldn't understand mom's resentment of my aunt but couldn't tell her or she would be upset at my disloyalty. Mom had married "Dear Gerald" who was adored by his four younger sisters. His first marriage ended in divorce so when he met and married mom he was excommunicated from the Catholic Church. My aunts never forgave her from "taking Gerald from the church". I doubt it ever occurred to them he chose to marry my mother.

Our two families ate all meals together at a huge table. Each morning mom clucked with disdain as my cousins used the same knife first to dab peanut butter and then gobs of jelly on their toast. They made a mess and by the end of the meal the abstract composition of peanut butter and jelly had to be scraped off the table. For fifteen years my mom continued to set out two separate knives each morning. "Oh, Evelyn," Ruthie laughed. "Why waste an extra knife." Ruthie

71

stated her feelings and you could accept them or not, it didn't matter to her. She laughed if you disagreed with her and said you'd see the light someday. What annoyed mom most was Ruthie and her three sisters always running to church and saying God would take care of everything.

I couldn't understand the intense resentment mom felt toward my aunts, not realizing their total non-acceptance of her. I found them dull but harmless. But I always had to agree with her and take her side or her feelings would be hurt and I would be punished by her withdrawal and silence. So for two weeks every summer I was torn between not taking mom's side and wanting to join in the laughter and silliness prevalent in our vacation home each day. Laughter was rarely a presence in our home. I was always astonished that my cousins could laugh with their mom and dad about everything.

Ruthie's year-round home was in an expensive suburban town where she had countless friends. A formal bridge luncheon for "the girls" consisted of cold cuts and a salad and mis-matched paper plates and napkins tossed onto a slightly stained tablecloth. An ever-present cocoon of cobwebs swayed through the glass chandelier which hung over the dining room table. Hemline sagging and hair drooping, she was the perfect hostess, joking and cajoling, jabbing the air with her cigarette to make a point. Everyone loved her.

I remembered our last phone conversation about a year ago."I'm seventy-eight and still running out in my high heels to sell real estate, Ger. Can't let this osteoporosis get me down, and I have to look pretty. It's not good with Uncle Herm. He's not exactly got Alzheimers but it's pretty close to it. He can't drive, and I go everywhere with him. He really shouldn't be alone too long. He forgets you know." There wasn't a hint of anger or self-pity in her voice. "It's hard. We have to repeat the same thing over and over. He loses things so we have three of everything now—his favorite mug, the car keys, anything important to him. Makes life easier and the kids are good. We just laugh and try to get him to understand. I think we're doing a pretty good job."

"There's lots of times I get upset; sometimes I get mad; sometimes I have unhappy thoughts. But you know what? I just pull out the happy thoughts and memories and they chase the bad, feelings away."

She giggled. "You know what I think of most often. I think of my honey coming to get me for a date. He wore a bright orange sweater and knickers and I thought he was the most beautiful thing in the world." She laughed again. "I'm so happy I have only great thoughts to remember. All those great pictures." We talked a few minutes longer and then, "Ok, Ger, have to go now and take care of

Uncle Herm. Hope it's not ten years before we talk again. See you hon." And she was gone.

I returned and knelt at the casket, stroking Ruthie's stone hand with a silent thank you filled with love. Her gifts of laughter, faith and hope filled my empty soul for two weeks every summer and, slowly over the years, without my ever knowing it, had become a part of me.

INSECURITIES

It happened again. I just returned from two glorious weeks of loafing on Cape Cod and all my complexes were reactivated because I didn't have an alligator emblem on my shirt. The town in which we rent a summer cottage has a large proportion of affluent summer residents. Even though I pride myself on not being concerned with appearances, when I return home each summer I feel totally insecure for at least two weeks. Everyone, from schoolboys who choose from a fleet of boats to sail to the retired executives who drive their Mercedes to pick up the Boston Globe or Wall Street Journal, wears Izod Lacoste knit shirts. The alligator snaps at me for two weeks wherever I go and the penguin on my pocket peers back dolefully.

Mothers wealthier than I appear different somehow. They seem impervious to the weather, difficult children or situations faced by middle-class wives like me. They walk in the same sand and dust that I do, but I swear their feet don't get dirty. When the temperature soars, they don't sweat. They might perspire a little, but they never sweat. And they don't yell at their kids in the supermarket either.

The first day of vacation I stood in the wine and cheese shop deciding whether I should spend an extra $5. on wine. The woman next to me ordered $100 worth of seafood canapés for a cocktail party. The blonde in the next row at the ball game wears the same wrinkled polo shirt and white shorts that I do, but there's a difference. She looks athletic; I look sloppy. Even their laundry has class. I sit bedraggled in the laundromat in my last set of clean clothes and watch enviously as the unwilted sophisticate next to me tosses her nautical designer sheets into the dryer.

We're proud of our fourteen-foot boat we brought with us this year so we could do some fishing and putt proudly toward Nantucket Sound. But mostly we stay busy dodging the wakes from a parade of Boston Whalers headed for deep-water fishing. The Bud Lite and ham sandwiches in our cooler provide a sad contrast to the gourmet lunches I'm sure are neatly packed aboard their boats in beautiful designer picnic baskets.

The glowing matron next to me in the supermarket line makes me feel like throwing a beach blanket over my head. Dressed in immaculate tennis togs, she wears an expensive sweater knotted carefully around her neck, casually perfect. I'm on my way home from clamming clad in faded shorts and a Red Sox tee shirt with a fishy smelling sweatshirt tied around my waist. The woman in the gift shop makes out a check for $75 for a shimmering mobile of glass starfish as I grab my son's arm muttering, "I'll kill you if you touch anything".

What am I doing here? All the women in this town seem to have curly hair, beautiful skin and lovely figures. It's like a movie. The damp wind brings a glow to their tanned faces. I get pale and cold and the ever-multiplying gray in my hair sticks up like Brillo. Is this self-abuse worth it? You bet. To me, this town of sun, sand and sea is my idea of heaven. I'll gladly unpack my imagined (?) inadequacies for another two weeks to be able to enjoy it again next summer.

August 1983

REACHING FORTY-FIVE

I've always been happy when my birthday rolled around because it was a day to celebrate and reassess where my life was headed. Thirty was ok. By marrying young, I felt as if there had been much emotional growth in the ten years since I became a bride. Even thirty-five wasn't bad. I experienced my first pregnancy and looked forward to a new phase of life. Forty was an important birthday. My daughter started school and my two sons were old enough to be self-sufficient and also help me. "Life begins at forty" held every promise.

Then I was going to be forty-five. For the first time in my life I didn't want to celebrate a birthday. I didn't want to be forty-five—five years away from fifty. All of a sudden fifty sounded old and I felt as if I was starting on the downhill swing of life, a place I didn't want to be.

But that was a while ago and during that time I've discovered that being forty-five is a pretty comfortable place to be. My knees and stomach droop a little more; veins and spots are more prominent and I wish they weren't, but I don't feel as if I'm going to seed. I'm not fighting age (not too hard anyway), just accepting my appearance while trying to look my best. I used to tsk,tsk at women who spent time in beauty parlors for perms and hair coloring. Now I join them. The "attractive mature woman" is rather how I would like to picture myself for a while.

There's an ease about life that wasn't present before, an acceptance of what is and not constantly wishing for how it should be. I call myself a cynical idealist and leave it at that. It's not that I especially like the "system", but have learned to work within and around it in a way that suits me. My values and principles haven't changed, they're still often contrary to the majority, but no longer do I spend feverish hours trying to convince you that my point of view is right. Now I can say with ease, "ok that's how you feel".

I hope my children have noticed a mellowing in my attitudes because it's there. I won't compromise values I cherish and hope to pass on to them, but try more gently to point out why my feelings are important rather than "you better think this way because I'm your mother". When my daughter wants to wear what I consider a bizarre outfit, I can say go ahead without preaching how foolish I think the style is. She's neat and clean, a good girl and I know this phase will pass. It's easier for both of us.

It's a delight to watch my two sons mature, apparently having assimilated most of the basic ethics and faith I've tried to impart to them. I know they live in a totally different world from the one in which I spent my teens and realize that many compromises are needed in order to survive, but it's reassuring to know they have a core of values on which to draw to help them cope with life. The most joyful moments of parenthood for me are as I watch my children implement ideals I feel are vital to becoming a good, caring person.

My children have experienced the death of all their grandparents within the past few years, a difficult time for our family. Yet this pain drew us closer together. They learned how to pitch in and help unselfishly through long, heartbreaking months of illness. They helped each other draw on hidden strengths and share in a commitment of love. I became acutely aware of my own mortality and underwent a deep re-evaluation on the direction and meaning of my own life.

Even in death, though, there can be growth and benefits. We sorely miss the faces of our loves ones around the dining room table, especially at holiday time and they can never be replaced. But these places are being filled by members of a new, extended family. It's been a joy to reach out to others who are alone or whose family has diminished to unite and share new traditions, warmth and love.

I think sustaining a successful marriage where both partners can continue to grow and share is one of life's most difficult jobs. My husband and I have had rocky times over the years as countless others have, but there's something quite wonderful and reassuring to have an emotional, physical and spiritual communion with a mate of almost twenty-five years and the realization that whatever the future holds our love can surmount any crisis.

So being forty-five isn't bad after all. The blunt edges of life have smoothed out a little and it's easier to get through the day. I'm looking forward with great joy and hope to the next forty-five years!

February 1984

SUNDAY SAILORS

If you think all the crazy drivers in New Jersey are on the road, then you've never seen the traffic on our waterways. Since no license is required to pilot, navigate or sail a boat, no qualifications are necessary and believe me, it's obvious. A visit to the municipal launching ramp at the Atlantic Highlands Marina offers the opportunity to view a continuing performance of inept seamanship. Pull up a beach chair, stretch out in the sun with a soda and sandwich and you'll be provided with a day's entertainment free of charge.

It's a busy ramp with lines of RVs, trucks and vans whose owners are lined up waiting to plunk their boat into the bay. Of course everyone wants to be first. The smell of burning rubber fills the air from the smoking rear tires of vehicles as they strain to pull boat and trailer out of the water. Someone trying to help often falls off the trailer and soon surfaces sputtering and swearing. Car engines overheat from the struggle, all motion comes to a halt and the line gets longer with impatient mariners waiting for another incompetent to get off the ramp and out of their way.

There doesn't seem to be a question of priorities for many of the sailors. They seem more concerned about having an ample supply of six-packs than they are about the number of life jackets or survival equipment aboard.

Boats often fly off the trailers into the water, smack into the one launched right before them—often a bigger or newer craft—and then the fun begins. The policeman who watches from a discrete distance is pressed into service once again. The most depressing sound is the glub, glub, glub heard after a nifty boat slides off the trailer ramp, hits the bay and rapidly fills with oily water. Someone forgot to put the drain plug in. So much for the day's outing.

Domestic dramas are played out every day. A husband and wife were launching their vessel when suddenly the trailer slipped and the wheel ran over her foot. "Stupid," he yelled, "why did you let go of the rope?"

"Nuts to your boat," she screamed, crying in pain. "How about my foot; I think it's broken."

"I don't care about your foot. I'm just afraid the propeller bent when it scraped bottom and they're damn expensive to replace."

"That's nothing," chimed in an old-timer. "We anchored in shallow water yesterday and I put on my waders to fix the shear pin. Some clown passed too close and his wake filled up the waders so fast I couldn't move an inch. Had to cut the darn things off with my fishing knife before I drowned. Now I need about $70 for a new pair."

"You think that's bad. My son was out in his speedboat last week going full throttle when he hit a sandbar and went flying over the windshield. He seems to be ok except for a miserable headache he can't shake off."

One gentleman attired in impeccable sailing attire was trying to put up the sail on his thirty-five foot sailboat while still in the launching area. "I hear you're sailing to Cape Cod," commented the grizzled fisherman next to me. "Have a lot of experience on the open ocean?"

"Heavens, no. My family and I only sail on weekends and usually stay here in the bay."

"Oh. How do you manage when you hit bad weather?"

"We never sail in foul weather. We only sail when the sun shines," he grinned. Did he make it to Cape Cod.? Of course. Doesn't God watch over fools and Sunday sailors?

SEPTEMBER RENEWAL

I sit on my back steps with a sandwich for lunch and inhale the beautiful day that surrounds me. Blue jays squawk and splash at the birdbath; squirrels chase each other in endless circles around the base of the maple tree. A fragile Monarch butterfly floats across the yard. Yellowing leaves from the birch tree brush by my face and land next to me, announcing that fall is near.

This fresh coolness is a respite from endless humid, polluted air which has choked and immobilized us. September is always the beginning of a new year for me and this day is an affirmation of my feeling of renewal. I feel refreshed after summer vacation, ready to meet the challenges of my "new" year. My family is out fishing, squeezing in a final day of fun before the colder weather arrives. Soon they'll return and the hum and rhythm of my life will pick up again. I don't feel guilty sitting here; I realize the need to enjoy such a special time and say "thanks God" for making it possible.

Patches of brown lawn have turned green again after constant watering and care. Bright yellow mums planted last week reach to the sun and fill the yard with their glow. Impatiens are bushier, their petals a rich salmon color. Bushes that drooped all summer now stand erect. The plants want a second chance, a final opportunity to strut their colors. "We're still vibrant; you haven't seen us at our best yet!"

Beyond the trees the noise of the Parkway traffic vibrates through the clear air and a new office building under construction at the edge of the cemetery abutting our property insults me. Its stark facade is an intruder against the soft green silhouette of the trees in my yard. I remember when I could look out my kitchen window and see only green. Now a new warehouse creeps closer to me, its monolithic presence choking my privacy as each new stage is added to the construction. I'd like to be able to flee to a place where no huge buildings intrude yet I know this is where I must make my home. My husband's job and the best educational opportunities for my children are here.

I block out the vision of tall buildings and the roar of traffic and focus on the soft sunlight filtering through the leaves onto baskets of ferns hanging on the fence. This yard is my oasis. I come here to seek peace during times of stress and fatigue and be renewed and strengthened by the timelessness of nature's kaleido-scope of changing colors and patterns.

We cannot run. We need to find our refuge whether relaxing with a book in a favorite chair, a shared cup of tea with a friend at the kitchen table, standing at the workbench in the cellar or harvesting the last crops from the garden. Then we can carry peace and renewal within our hearts as we face each day.

September 1985

ODE TO THE BURGER FLIPPERS

I recently saw a program on public television where panelists discussed the controversy regarding the validity of College Board SAT scores and the pressure placed on high school students to qualify for admission to prestigious universities. One student's father expressed serious concern to his son that the last thing he wanted him to become was a "burger flipper".

Of course we need CEOs, college presidents and computer experts, but without the employees in our service industries, the so called "burger flippers", many of whom are not college graduates, we wouldn't have a functioning society. It's past time to question the arrogant attitude of those whose only measure of success is title and salary and to acknowledge and respect the middle class which allows our country to function successfully. They are the backbone of our country.

College is not for everyone. Approximately one-third of entering freshmen graduate from universities and many obtain positions not even closely related to their college major. In the resort town where I live, a large number of successful college graduates, some who earned six-figure incomes in successful but unrewarding careers, have returned to their roots and become builders, landscapers and craftsmen.

Consider a few major areas in the lives of most American families: their homes, their cars, and leisure and entertainment. Try to eliminate the non-degree employees who contribute to our happiness and welfare: the countless craftsmen who build our homes; electricians, plumbers and appliance repairmen who respond to our frantic telephone calls; the farmers, truck drivers and supermarket employees who provide food for our tables.

Americans enjoy a love affair with their cars. Eliminate those who produce, sell, repair and maintain them. Status can't be achieved if there's no one to assemble that luxury sedan or SUV. We need all employees involved in supplying gas to service stations and don't forget the owners of auto body and repair shops.

More families enjoy traveling each year. Think of everyone who makes sure you get to your destination: travel and airline reservation agents, baggage handlers, food preparation staff and flight mechanics. Without them there would be no jumbo-jet flights, no get-away, exciting vacations. Who would staff cruise ships bound for exotic ports around the world? Most popular resorts including Disneyworld and Universal Studios would be forced to close down.

Leisure and entertainment—when families can relax and re-connect with each other. Working moms have little time or energy to prepare family dinners during the week. The magic words are "take-out". What if all fast-food and take-out establishments—from the Golden Arches to a trendy deli in Manhattan closed their doors? Or the local pizzeria or Chinese restaurant didn't provide delivery service any longer. Then what's for dinner? American families eat out approximately twice a week. Whether you're headed for a five star restaurant or Burger King, who's going to produce, cook and serve your meal?

Family life would change drastically. Most day-care centers are run by teachers who are college graduates. However, their aides, the backbone of the programs, sometimes don't possess a college degree. Baby-sitters, nannies and the men and women employed to clean millions of homes often haven't attended college. Remove these folks from the workplace and it's impossible to imagine the impact on working mothers and their families.

So the next time you're tempted to scoff at someone because they haven't attended or graduated from college, stop and think again. Do a mental check on what service that person provides to make life easier for you. Perhaps someday in our society after being introduced to a new acquaintance, the first question asked will not be—"what do you do"—but instead—"who are you".

February 2001

MR. B.

I approached the Boy Scout leader with apprehension, my mind cluttered with the resentment I sometimes felt when I needed someone to help my son. The noisy, boisterous swirl of the Boy Scouts in the room reinforced my feeling that I was making a mistake by enrolling Kevin in the troop. His Cub Scout years had been spent with a den mother who was an understanding friend. Since my husband's work schedule didn't allow him to participate in Scout activities, now Kevin would be with indifferent strangers.

Mr. B. listened quietly as I explained Kevin's learning disabilities, severe asthma, and the fact he was always the "goat" in any group, never accepted by his peers. I disliked asking for special consideration for him, but years of experience had taught me it was best to be honest with people. I hoped would be able to help him grow and mature.

"He'll be ok, dearie. You just run along now and pick him up when the meeting's over." Mr. B. smiled gently, patting my arm as he peered at me over the rim of his glasses. I didn't believe him.

"Mr. B.", Gerry Batchelder has been the Scoutmaster of Troop 68 at Connecticut Farms Church in Union, NJ for more than twenty years. He's fostered the growth of a countless number of boys, but I'm sure he hasn't done a better job with anyone than he has with my two sons. He, more than anyone, through example, "friendly persuasion", and his quiet way, has helped them to become fine young men. As their friend and Scout leader he imbued in them a sense of responsibility and loyalty that I still find surprising. Their dedication to him is complete. Eight years is a long time—the years between ten and eighteen when a boy is developing into a young man and his world is changing daily. Those are the years he's been there to guide my boys.

Soon Kevin was selling candy and light bulbs to raise money for the troop, enjoying himself at holiday parties and helping out at paper and aluminum drives. "It's ok, mom. Mr. B. will be there," was the reassurance he gave me whenever he saw the familiar worried look on my face. There were still hassles with some boys who considered him the oddball, but Mr. B. explained Kevin's problems and for the first time he became part of a group.

Since his chronic asthma was severely aggravated by cold weather, Kevin had stayed close to home during the winter months. Now he became involved in the Klondike Derby, an all-day outdoor competition in midwinter among the many troops from the Watchung Council. "I have to help Mr. B.", he grinned as he bundled up and hurried out the door. For the first time, Kevin spent a weekend away from home on a Scout camping trip. "I'll just take my pills and I'll be fine, mom. Don't worry about it." What magic did this man work with my son?

The spring after Kevin joined the troop, Mr. B. and I stood at the back of town hall waiting for the Township Committee meeting to begin. The scouts marched in to present the colors and lead the opening exercises. "Salute", Kevin beamed proudly as he shouted the word. To my stutterer who had special education assistance and speech therapy for years, this one word uttered before an audience was a monumental step.

Mr. B., clad in his red jacket and standing a distance from me, nodded and winked in his impish way, "I told you so", written across the grin on his face. With one success story behind him, was he ready for my younger son, Christopher?

"I'm not wearing that monkey suit for anybody and I don't want to be a stupid Boy Scout," Chris ranted as he got ready for his first scout meeting. Although gifted in many ways, he projected a false bravado and an "I don't care" attitude to hide his gentleness and insecurities.

Before long though, Chris was responding to Mr. B. without even being aware of it. Fiercely competitive, he sold extra candy for fundraisers, collected donations for the cancer fund and culminated his achievements by signing up the largest number of sponsors for the annual ten-mile Victory Hike. By raising the most money of any scout in the Watchung Council, he won first prize—the television set which still sits in his room.

Neither Chris nor Kevin seemed able to recount what was discussed in their lengthy conversations with Mr. B. "Nothing much", was the usual answer, but I noted a growing respect for the man, an eager willingness to volunteer and help whenever he needed an extra hand. "Mr. B. needs us, mom." That was it.

Chris was an usher at church for Scout Sunday, participated in the Flag Day ceremony and marched in the Memorial Day parade. My shy introvert was now proud to wear his uniform. He rose through the ranks and was on his way toward becoming an Eagle Scout.

Mr. B. was there when Chris went to summer camp, offering encouragement and support. He took him to counselor's homes in order to pass various merit badge tests. He helped him organize special projects and kept pushing and encouraging him to reach within himself to discover his potential.

Two years ago my mom and mother-in-law became bedridden with cancer at the same time. For those two years, Mr. B. was there. He drove the boys to and from meetings and all special activities. A secure haven for them, he often stopped for pizza or burgers on the way home. He was there, listening, loving and trying to help them understand the confusion and grief they felt.

Often he shared a cup of coffee with my husband and me. Although we talked many hours, I never really got to know him. A shy, private man, his goodness and actions spoke for him.

In June, Chris became an Eagle Scout. As I look at the proud, smiling faces in the snapshots taken that night, I whisper a silent thank you to Mr. B. for helping my sons draw upon inner resources they never realized they possessed to enable them to grow and become all they could be.

June 1984

THANKSGIVING

Serendipity: "The gift of finding valuable or agreeable things not sought for." One of my favorite words reminds me again that there can be a pleasant surprise or positive aspect to almost every situation if we look hard enough. Perhaps it's been an entire year you'd like to forget, but Thanksgiving is the time to poke around for positives. You might be surprised at what you find.

Our kids often drive us crazy. We always seem to be driving them somewhere, waiting for appointments, hurrying to speed them on their way to becoming adults. Why not say thanks to those who help them through the maze of childhood and adolescence: Scout leaders who spend hours planning meetings, special events and camping trips; religious education teachers who volunteer their time to help our kids become caring, concerned people; coaches who help them realize their potential in athletics and instill a sense of sportsmanship and camaraderie.

I'm fortunate to have a job I enjoy, a boss with integrity who treats me with consideration and kindness and co-workers it's a pleasure to greet each morning. We disagree at times and get on each other's nerves, but I think I'm lucky. One co-worker talks incessantly but the guy at the next desk brings me coffee each day. That's the way it goes.

I have friends and neighbors who are always there when I need them. They collect packages from the UPS man, bring in the garbage cans twice a week or drive me fifteen miles to pick up my husband's set of keys at work after I lock myself out of the house. It's a glorious feeling to know I can pick up the phone and receive help immediately. I'm spoiled, for there aren't too many neighborhoods like mine anymore.

Thanks to the priests who lead my church community in the search for peaceful solutions to the problems of mankind. Their job isn't an easy one. To keep perspective while not losing their smile, to console others when they may be hurting more, to inspire faith when theirs may be lagging. Then comes the joy of mass, baptism, communion or confirmation and my faith is reaffirmed again.

Thanks to my three kids for putting up with my ever-changing moods. I tell them all geniuses are moody and they just laugh. To a daughter who patiently keeps trying to help me look "jazzy". To three super kids who leave books, sneakers and socks strewn around the first floor all week but help me vacuum and dust each Saturday. For two sons who cleaned up the house and prepared a tasty Italian meal for us after their dad and I returned from a long weekend. They tell me I look pretty as I leave for a wedding reception . They encourage my writing and leave me alone when I want solitude. They hug me every day.

Most of all this holiday I'm thankful for my husband. We've been married a long time and will always be in the process of "adjusting". He's a man who does the grocery shopping, laundry and cooking. A considerate man who sorts out the mess I've made of our checkbook and takes time to prepare a huge antipasto for a friend's surprise birthday dinner. He's a gentle man who could always fix the barrette in Nancy's hair or tie the bow in her dress better than I could.

He still gets a hug and "good night dad" from adult sons even after bellowing at them over dinner because they know how much he cares. He's a man who surprises me with a bowl of flowers and a lovely note on the kitchen table after a stormy argument. I am blessed. So are you. Look around.

November 1985

THANKSGIVING II

The best Thanksgiving celebrations I remember as a kid were the ones we shared with my mom's aunt and uncle, Mildred and Frank. There was lots of laughter and noise in the house, I was able to see forbidden pictures and eat all the after-dinner mints I could stuff down my throat. The rest of the year I spent every Sunday visiting my two sets of grandparents, aunts, uncles and cousins with my mom, dad and brother. It was awful. No one laughed or told jokes; my mom was always after me to behave and I had to play stupid board games with my cousins.

Mildred and Frank's home was different. Their daughter, Doris, was my mom's best friend so I guess that's how we ended up there each Thanksgiving. They had many French Canadian relatives and friends who were full of fun and mischief. Uncle Frank, whose whiskey tumbler was always full, made sure his guests were never thirsty and they were delighted to join him. Their laughter grew more raucous and their songs louder as the day progressed. Only my family stayed for dinner. The rest moved on to nearby homes of other relatives for the turkey feast.

Mildred looked like her cats—or her cats looked like her. They were huge house cats with giant heads. Three of them, all with gray, white and black markings and sinister eyes that followed you from their perch on top of the guests' coats piled on the bed. Mildred's face was a perfect circle, her eyes tiny slits which never missed a trick. She always wore a thin hair net to cover her wispy white hair which clumped in puffs on top of her head right where a cat's ears would be. If she had her teeth in when she grinned, she was the perfect Cheshire cat.

There was a small alcove off the living room with shelves full of books and magazines. That's where I discovered National Geographic. I don't know how old I was when I first saw the naked women carrying water jars on their heads or babies on their backs but I remember thinking: jeez—is that what mom and my aunts look like underneath their dresses? Is that what I'm going to look like?

So the women chatted, chopped and peeled in the kitchen while the men sat around laughing and telling stories. I hid in my alcove, blocked from view by two over-stuffed chairs. After I got over my fascination with breasts, I discovered I could travel the world, come face to face with a grizzly or learn about the moon—all on these pages. I was in heaven with my mints and magazines.

Methodical Mildred put a huge bowl of after-dinner mints wrapped in shiny green paper on the same round table next to the alcove every year. We never had those at home. First I casually tried to take one at a time but this entailed too many trips out of my lair. Then I realized I could take half of them at once and carefully re-arrange the rest to make the bowl look full. Every year I thought I would get sick if I ate another one—but it never happened.

By dinnertime I wasn't hungry but had to choke down what mom put on my plate. I think my mom and dad enjoyed a little extra to drink on those Thanksgivings, perhaps making up for so many stilted Sundays. Doris acted as referee between her parents. Mildred was tired from days of preparation and yelled at Frank to carve the turkey. But he was tilted sideways in his armchair at the head of the table, snoring loudly, dreaming whiskey dreams. Mildred and Doris would pull him to the adjoining bedroom and flop him onto the bed with the coats and the cats. Everybody was happy and I think that's why my dad learned to carve a turkey.

DECISION

About ten years ago I was a Eucharistic Minister for my parish in New Jersey. This is a lay person who is allowed to distribute communion alongside the priest during mass and can also bring communion to someone who is ill at home or in the hospital. I felt proud and considered it an honor but there was always an underlying unease, a discomfort in this role.

Ever since I was a child I considered God my best friend and talked to Him daily. But as much as I loved the ritual of weekly mass and the feeling of belonging to a parish, the older I got the more I questioned the rules of the church and the authority of the Pope. Too many rules seemed to be church rules—not God's rules—and had nothing to do with being a good person.

I struggled with these feelings for years as I went to mass each Sunday with my family, became active in my parish and participated in a three-year course to become a lay minister. Ritual, tradition and the friendships formed through a wide variety of church activities helped fill a need, a void, through the passages of my life.

And then came this Easter Sunday. I stood at the altar with the other Eucharistic Ministers, waiting to share communion and looked into the faces of the people who packed the church. I felt like a hypocrite and a cheat. How could I share communion with them when I knew that increasingly I disagreed with more church rules and laws?

I distributed communion to the long lines of parishioners and was almost finished when the Superintendent of Schools stood in front of me. Since I was an employee of the school system he was my boss even though I seldom saw him. I had known him for years on a personal level and through those years had grown extremely disappointed and sometimes angry regarding his priorities as far as teachers and students were concerned.

I stared at him. The words and the realization—"Gerry, who are you to judge him or anybody? How do you know what pain this man has inside him, what makes him tick" jumped into my head and heart. Hand shaking, I handed the host to him.

Kneeling in the pew for final prayers as mass ended, I couldn't quiet the pounding inside me. I have never felt so humbled. And I have never gone back to mass.

More than ten years have passed since that Easter Sunday. Through the hardships and losses over the years, God has remained my steadfast best friend. When I enter a Catholic church for a wedding, funeral mass or perhaps a Christmas concert, I feel at home and still sometimes miss the ritual and richness the church offered me for many years. But the personal closeness I feel to God, the peace I feel within myself because I am being true to my beliefs and the knowledge that I am trying to be the best person I can be remind me again that my faith grows stronger every day.

February 2001

TURTLE EGGS IN THE DRIVEWAY

"Second house on right, American flag in front, watch for turtle eggs in driveway"—directions on the invoice slip for a delivery of lumber to our summer home on Cape Cod. Friends can't understand why we've vacationed on the Cape for twenty-five years and intend to retire here without visiting a variety of travel destinations. Where else would folks worry about turtle eggs?

We live in a town of 50,000 in New Jersey, a thirty minute drive to New York City. Fear has crept in slowly over the years. It's a town where you're wary at mini-malls after dark and always remember to set your car alarm. We've become inconsiderate, hostile and untrusting as we get caught in the temper and times of today's society. The Cape is our refuge.

The advertised allure of the Cape rests in the National Seashore, nature sanctuaries, artist's colonies and marvelous restaurants. But the residents and their acceptance and trust are the Cape's greatest natural resource. The shopkeeper who doesn't stock my stove replacement part but calls two competitors to find the item and hands me a map with directions to their shop. The check-out clerk at the A&P who says, "You don't have to bring in the mums from outside, just tell me how many pots you're taking".

Before the interstate was completed, a woman in Wareham took one look at our Beverly Hillbilles station wagon packed tight with kids and luggage, topped by a canoe and towing a boat full of fishing gear and decided we had sat long enough in summer traffic. "Going to the Cape? Follow me I'll show you a shortcut." We chased her down narrow, twisting back roads, through two church parking lots and the middle of a Fourth of July parade before she deposited us on Route 6. "There you go; have a great vacation."

When our car broke down on a desolate road in Truro, the tow truck driver brought along a friend with a van who transported the six of us back to the repair center. It was closing time on Thanksgiving eve but the mechanic sent his assistant to the next town for the needed part and bought us coffee and donuts. He repaired the car within a few hours at a reasonable price and showed a happy family the meaning of Thanksgiving.

A burly fisherman heard our sputtering boat motor as we prepared for a day of fishing. After checking it over he told us to wait, he'd be back with a part. Not only did he repair the motor but handed us his two-way radio in case we had trouble. Only ten minutes out the motor quit and we called him to ask for a tow. "Come on, I'll take you and the kids fishing. You sure don't want to spoil their day." So off we went with a new friend in his boat, a true hero to my kids.

"Bring the motor back tomorrow. I have a friend who can fix it for you." We returned the following morning and left the boat and motor at his cluttered shop. When we returned the motor was repaired, had been tuned up and sounded brand new—with no extra charge.

A few years ago we purchased two watercolor paintings from a local artist we knew who exhibited her work in our town's annual arts festival. Friends who were staying with us also purchased a painting and left for New Jersey the following morning. That night they called, asking us to purchase a companion painting to fill wall space larger than expected.

Unfortunately, the painting had been sold and we explained our dilemma to the artist. "Well, just stop at my home studio in Orleans. The door's open. Pick out whatever paintings you think your friends might like and take them back to New Jersey. When you come back to the Cape next month you can return the ones you don't want and pay me then."

Why would I want to live anywhere else?

Summer 1985

ON AWAKENING

You love yet don't respect me.
An annoyance, an inconvenience, an irritant—
who I am is not who you love.

Forty years of love and self-denial have
only returned me to the first day we met.

Fear and resentment prevent you from
joining me in new life, new beginnings.

I see the end of the road
and am eager to soar toward a destination
overflowing with postponed hopes and dreams.
To savor every minute as a gift.

Are you able to join me at last
or do I still travel alone?

1997

ARRANGING GLADIOLUS

I'm trying to arrange joyful gladiolus in a smooth, cream-colored bottle vase. Only two stalks—but they argue with me as usual. One spike is larger, a pale shrimp color. It is delicate but sturdy and stands regally. The smaller flower has splatters of crimson lining its pink ridges and tilts at an awkward angle.

The flowers refuse to cooperate as they spin, twist and stick in the bottle. I'm careful not to touch the fragile buds still to open as I struggle with the stems and realize that this is my life playing out in front of me. I notice the stronger stem is curved and bent at the bottom—hidden in the bottle. As we hide our twists and quirks beneath the surface.

The flowers push away from each other, two people—my husband and I, trying to connect; we want to but we can't. I nudge the flowers in a different direction, forcing them together in the bottle but they almost snap. They merge and then each leans in a different direction. I can't force this relationship; it wouldn't last.

I gently peel a leaf from one stem so it will not clog the bottle. Then another. Layer by layer I must strip away old pain, resentment, despair, anger. I have forgiven all a long time ago but my soul needs to forget.

A few drops of water drip from the bottle. Silent tears as we try to come together. Each time I move the vase the beautiful spikes of color re-arrange themselves. They face each other; then they turn away and twirl in opposite directions, reversing themselves to cling again. The opened blossoms are my life today. The tightly furled buds at the top of the stem, not yet ready to open, hold the promise of our life together.

Summer 1997

THE BEACH

I don't remember when my mom, dad, younger brother and I started to spend two weeks' vacation every summer at the New Jersey shore, but it's where I found my home. We stayed with my dad's sister, her husband and my three cousins at their new summer house. I found one snapshot of all the kids taken when I was about eight years old, but we vacationed there until I graduated from high school.

How long did it take me to realize that my aunt and uncle laughed at life every day with their children. We didn't do that at our house. That I was the oldest and expected to set a good standard for the rest of the kids. Unfortunately, being a rebel from a young age, I usually set a bad example and my mom was always on my case. She never wanted to be there for vacation and I felt disloyal when I didn't spend time with her, but she didn't like the beach so I was with my dad all the time. We were buddies. At the beach by nine, home by noon where he ate provolone and salami sandwiches every lunchtime on crunchy Italian bread. I don't remember what I ate. Back to the beach by one, home by four and then I always returned to the sea alone every evening after supper.

During the two-block walk back and forth and all our hours together dad and I hardly talked but it didn't bother me for he was a quiet man. But I do remember the wonderful times we bobbed in the waves, rode them in to shore and tumbled in the foam, finally surfacing, spitting sand. He would roar with laughter, hike up his bathing suit, grab my hand and head out for the next wave. When I was in the water I felt as if I was in heaven and truly close to God.

Scanning the horizon, I had visions of China at the outer edge. My mind was busy and every day I took a different journey to a far destination on the other side. Lying on the beach blanket, my fingers and hand smoothing the sand, I felt part of the earth. Standing at the water's edge, I felt powerful as my feet sank deeper and deeper into the sand as the incoming tide swirled around me. The beach, ocean and I were one.

I can't remember the rest of the family being at the beach with us but of course they were. I only recall one day after a hurricane, my brother, cousins and I were huddled high on a dune in a sand fort we had built, feeling very brave as the surging waves crashed around us. We were invincible. Until an unseen, unexpectedly huge wave tumbled over the top of us and sent us terrified and crying, flying down the street toward home.

My solitary walks each night after supper were wonderful. An empty beach, lots of shorebirds, a few fishermen—total peace. One damp night I was walking when it quickly became foggy. I felt totally alone gliding along on a silent magic carpet of sand. As the mist swirled around, I caught a glimpse of twinkling bright colored stars far off in the distance. I felt lighter than air, suspended in my own world. Then I realized my stars were lights from the rides on the amusement pier a few miles down the beach.

That night I couldn't wait to get home to write down my magical feelings so I wouldn't forget them. Fifty years later, I'm still recording how the feelings, tastes, smells and the enduring joy of beach walks continue to nourish my soul.

October 1999

SOARING SIXTIES

Monday I was sixty years old. It was the best birthday I ever had and I am on my way! They told me "life begins at forty" but since I have usually described my life as controlled chaos, I figured I would be late getting started—but not twenty years late. This celebration is a true epiphany.

Flowers from family and friends fill the rooms of my home. I touch each of the arrangements every time I pass and feel love in velvet petals. Cards are lined up on my windowsills and I grin each time I see them. Many included letters and photos and I toasted each sender with a cup of tea in my kitchen as I felt their presence with me. I was delighted to find quirky, loving, animated and musical cards on my e-mail in the morning. My children and some friends sang "happy birthday" over the phone. I loved every minute.

For my birthday I went to the National Seashore to hear a fascinating lecture about owls. Then the movie, "Shakespeare in Love", a wonderful dinner and a glass of wine at a favorite restaurant and then home. I was alone but surrounded by joy and love.

My health keeps improving. My writing is going well; ideas tumble out on top of each other all day long and I can't get them down fast enough. The spiritual core I thought was lost is slowly growing stronger. I have tried, at last, to stop giving my husband and children advice which will help improve their lives. Best of all—I finally like me.

The biggest surprise was a knock on my front door late that night. It was my husband. He didn't tell me he was coming from New Jersey, perhaps because I might say no. He wanted to spend this special birthday with me. We spent three glorious days getting re-acquainted, doing a lot arguing, crying and loving. Our time spent apart has given us many months to do a lot of thinking and we are ready to re-build a new marriage. I know the path will be difficult and often stormy because that's who we are. But my heart tells me that the healthier, stronger love we are building will allow me to spend my days with the man I truly love.

February 1999

MOON AND STARS

I just finished the first class of an eight-week course in astronomy held at the library and I'm back in outer space for the first time in countless years. The description in the brochure for "backyard astronomy" leads me to believe that since no math or measuring instruments are involved, this is something I will be able to understand.

On my way home with a head full of information on exploding stars, the alignment of planets and where to look for them in the sky, I pass right by my street and forget to turn. I'm really not in my car, though; I'm ten years old and back in my childhood home staring at the moon through my bedroom window.

"Only jerks sit staring at the moon, Gerry. Go to sleep." My eight year old brother who shares the bedroom with me is logical and concise and has no romance in his soul. "Just shut up; I'll sit here as long as I want to." What's out there I wonder. Everything and nothing is out there. I know God is out there only I don't mention that to anybody. Ever since I first looked up at the night sky it has fascinated me. There are so many stars. Many moonless nights I sat at my bedroom window amazed that the longer I sat there, more stars kept appearing. Where did they keep coming from?

Tonight is a hot oppressive August night and the heavy smell of honeysuckle from the vacant lot next door fills the room. I stare at the half-moon and wonder if people all over the world can see the moon at the same time I'm looking at it. People in China and at the North Pole. I like to think that everyone in the world can see it with me and feel connected to all of them in some way I don't understand.

How did God create this whole universe? I've only learned a little about the planets in 5th grade general science so I don't know much. Who first saw the planets and who gave them the names they have? I want to know everything there is to know about "out there" because it seems to me if I have that connection, in some way I'll understand God better and become a nicer person. The black expanse above my head filled with sparkling lights must hold the answers to every kind of question.

I didn't know much about our universe when I was ten, but I remember thinking then, as I do now, if we are here—others can be out there.

1-28-99

WINTER CLOUDS

Bitter black layers try to suffocate those below,
yet the pewter mass beneath struggles to catch the wind.

Slate slivers reach slowly toward the west
as alabaster wisps ease toward a horizon
eager for the healing rays of a winter sun

Then I realize—
strength can only come from my core
and rise.

February 1999

THE TREE

I love trees. Every kind of tree and everything about them. When I sit beneath one I love the feel of the rough bark against my back, my hands touching the solid roots beneath me and the lacy pattern of leaves above my head. It's a wonderful feeling of being one with the earth and universe at the same time when I look up at the strong branches reaching for the sun.

So after our last snowstorm I was devastated to see one of my favorite fir trees snapped in half from the weight of heavy wet snow. When Kevin, a huge, rough—looking man, came to cut off the top of the tree I couldn't watch when I heard his chainsaw whirring. Then a knock on the door. "Gerry, this pine tree next to it is dead and split in a lot of places. I really should take it down while I'm here."

Oh, no. The pine tree was next to "my tree" a medium sized oak just like the one in the backyard of my childhood home where I had spent countless hours reading, writing, watching clouds and dreaming. My paper dolls had unlimited adventures around its base where they could always return to a safe haven. It had been my refuge from all perceived and real hurts as I grew up.

Now, at our retirement home, my husband had wanted to cut off the bottom branches which were just a few feet from the ground because it was difficult to mow the grass beneath them. But I still wanted and needed those low branches to provide a cocoon for the days I sat beneath the tree. The pine Kevin wanted to cut down sat between the oak and fir and I knew its crashing limbs would crush and break many of my oak's branches.

"Well, could you be as careful as possible," I started hesitantly, realizing of course he was doing a difficult job and didn't need interference from me. What did a few branches matter? Then, before I could stop myself, I was chattering rapidly about how important the tree and its protective branches were to me, explaining childhood memories and the need for the tree to remain intact. Feeling foolish and embarrassed I finally stopped as I saw his expression change.

"No kidding," he replied with a wide grin. "I know exactly how you feel. When I was a kid we had a lot of land behind our house which led down to a stream. Right by the steam there was a hollow in the ground; we never did figure out how it got that way. That's where I used to play with my toy soldiers all the time because it was warm and sunny. I loved that spot so much that when I was little and took a nap my mom would let me take my sleeping bag down there and that's where I'd sleep. It was great. I can almost feel the roll of the ground right now. Say, don't worry about the tree." He patted my shoulder and returned to work.

I waited until the roar of the saw stopped and heard his truck pull away before I could look out the window. The branches now had more room to spread out and the cocoon I cherished invited me back. My oak stood strong.

4-8-99

SPRING DAY

Dangling prisms refract comets of color and hope
across stark walls of my kitchen and heart.

The cat stalks a rabbit which becomes
a frozen statue hidden behind red tulips.

Squirrels and jays battle at the feeder.

The phone——
death of a friend, prayers for my daughter,
my husband's soft voice.

Mail——
hope for a cancer patient, birth of a baby.

I write—
Letters, essays, a poem.

Late rays of sun slant through the window
and form a golden orb of promise
enveloping daffodils in a green bowl.

Light rests on forsythia reaching for joy
from a vase in a corner of the room.

This beauty existed last spring but was unseen;
today I taste peace.

4-8-99

COLUMBINE CARNAGE—THE DAY AFTER

The morning after the carnage at Columbine High School I sought answers in nature. At a herring run where the fish had started their spring migration from Cape Cod Bay upstream to a quiet pool where they would spawn. There were many small herring but rather than trying to leap up the ladders of tumbling water to their destination, they huddled together in a quiet eddy, all facing downstream. Perhaps children afraid to face the future. Circling, squawking seagulls overhead searched for weak or dead fish for breakfast. They seemed to represent the threatening adult world.

The carnage at Columbine was still etched in my brain from television images the previous night. I couldn't understand two things: why are we surprised that this horror has occurred and why, according to the countless counselors, psychiatrists, law enforcement experts and school administrators interviewed do we need "to reach the children". The focus instead should be on us, the adults who created the social environment in which we live. The killers were in many ways influenced by negative principles and values of our society we don't wish to acknowledge or discuss.

We've allowed more than a generation of children to be raised on a steady accepted diet of violence through television, video and computer games, music and movies. As adults we pay millions at the box office to see violence and gore. Daily, these children have become de-sensitized to repeated acts of violence which are depicted as accepted ways of solving a problem. If confronted with a difficult situation or an annoying or threatening person just "blow them away". It seems to be the American way.

In a society where the chasm between wealthy and poor continues to widen at a steady pace, there will be more disaffected children. Lonely boys and girls raised in broken homes or homes in which they see or are subjected to repeated occasions of verbal, emotional or physical abuse will find each other for acceptance and security. Their friends become family.

It did not surprise me the gunmen singled out "jocks" as targets. As a nation we worship professional athletes, some of whom receive only a slap on the wrist for serious drug, alcohol and family abuse offenses. Above the law or values we supposedly hold important, they are a vital cog on a team that must win at any cost. Sports stars and celebrities in the entertainment field are our national heroes, not teachers, ministers or artists.

Neither did it surprise me that they targeted a student of color. We are a racist society. Minorities are threatened by an influx of new minority groups seeking refuge in our country. We form committees, hold open forums and meetings to discuss the problem of racial equality and harmony. But many white Americans who work with minorities daily and share lunch, dinner out or a drink after work are the first to flee their neighborhood when the same co-worker buys a home on their street. "They" are moving in.

Additional security in our schools will not change the attitudes students bring to school with them each day. Children are sponges, soaking up the conversation, principles and tenor of their homes. No metal detector alters the inherent values students have learned from their parents, many of whom who do not their children as a priority but have a desperate need to be the first, the best or have the most for themselves.

Is success only a corner office, a huge salary, expensive vacations or a bigger car? Does it mean we must be puppets answering beepers, cell phones and e-mail so we're not out of the loop? We worship computers which diminish human interaction and we fill day care centers with children who are programmed to achieve before birth. Many people with high incomes, marvelous careers and good health still feel unfulfilled, a restlessness, an unease. Something is missing at the core of our society; it's hard to give it a name. Money and technology are not filling a human void.

A man stood next to me this morning as his toddler splashed with fascination at the bubbling pool of herring. Questions about fish, bubbles and stones tumbled out of the boy in a torrent. The man never answered his son; he couldn't hear him. He was still on his cell phone as he pulled the crying, protesting child back to the car.

April 21, 1999

FEAR OF FLYING

Over capricious sheets of foam
Flight I ache to share

Feet planted on a sturdy board,
the windsurfer's lone translucent wing
grabs the wind

Soars—flies—leap-frogs
across roiling steel-gray seas

Racing clouds to the horizon.

October 1999

SKIN DEEP

I finally discovered that the polluted, grimy air which hovers over my hometown in New Jersey is actually good for something. It has helped to keep me looking young.

Before I retired, during discussions at work we often compared the variety of skin creams, cleansers, purifiers, facial masks and eye creams available for either day or nighttime use. I usually kept silent. I did not share my co-workers enthusiasm for spending large amounts of money on lotions and potions guaranteed to stop the aging process. These dollars only fill the coffers of a clever inflation and recession-proof cosmetics industry since the variety and cost of anti-aging potions increases daily. Miracle agents are listed for morning and afternoon application, oily, dry and normal skin, and for wrinkles and creases above, below and on the sides of the eyes and mouth.

Who can keep track of and remember in which order and how these items are to be applied to the skin? Instead of a morning or afternoon coffee break, women will need a "freshen-up" break when they hurry off to the rest room and apply the appropriate creams depending on whether it is nine, ten or eleven am.

I've been told "for your age, you have a lovely complexion". I smile and say thank you and hope they don't ask the next question—"what do you use on your face?" since I don't like to lie. I smile and acknowledge I usually use soap and warm water. They glance slyly since they know there has to be a battery in my arsenal to achieve my perceived youthful appearance. I can't tell them the truth. I just gently scrub my face with warm water and apply a light film of Vaseline some evenings. Blasphemy.

Returning to Cape Cod from New Jersey this week, I discovered that my daughter, twenty-four and without a wrinkle, could open a beauty supply shop using what she has stacked on our bathroom shelves. Items with names like "Serious Body Moisture", "Prevent and Correct Lotion", "Lip Zone Anti-Feathering Complex", and the best—"Oxygenating Fluid"—which sounded like an additive for my car's fuel tank. I decided to experiment and indulge myself in a "thorough cleansing of the pores and rough, dry skin" as directed on the label. My choice was an apricot and sea kelp facial scrub. Smelled good, seemed harmless.

I followed the directions exactly and after patting my face dry, applied the appropriate dab of face cream which was called for at 9:45 p.m. My cheeks felt so soft I must admit I was surprised and delighted. Then I put on my glasses. What happened? I didn't recognize the crone in the mirror who stared back at me. Where did she come from? I cleaned the spots off my eyeglasses and stared again. It was worse. My cheeks did have a deep, rosy glow, but I rather resembled a clown and looked ten years older. Pale age spots had darkened and multiplied. Ones that were dime-sized were now worth a quarter. Bags beneath my eyes suddenly drooped an extra inch. The creases around my eyes indicated an extremely large crow had probably been standing on my face for a long time. The lines which pulled down from my mouth gave me the appearance of a ventriloquist's dummy.

For the first time my face had been totally cleansed and the effect was horrifying. It was at that moment I realized that the accumulated toxins in the New Jersey air probably had held my face together all these years and provided a veneer which covered a multitude of flaws. I had allowed them to accumulate slowly, never having sand-blasted them off my face until now with disastrous results.

So the next time I drive back to New Jersey from the Cape, when I reach the Connecticut Turnpike I'll have to open all the car windows to enable enough air to flow through in order to re-finish my complexion so friends will recognize me when I arrive.

Spring 1999

ROLE MODELS

Tuesday night was my first night as a teacher's aide in an English as a Second Language class for adults at Dennis-Yarmouth Regional High School. I only help out on Tuesday but the students have been attending three-hour classes two nights a week since September and will continue until the regular school year is over in June. George, the teacher, reminded them they have to show up through the cold winter months because if they don't there's a waiting list of 400 ready to take their place in the classroom.

The group I enjoyed being with a few years ago understood very little English and most evenings we worked with basic picture dictionaries, survival skill words with much mime and gesturing. This new group of students has been enrolled in classes for the past few years and their command of English is much stronger. Most are Brazilian immigrants who speak Spanish or Portuguese who have moved to the Cape and taken jobs in service industries in order to start a new life. I don't know the backgrounds of my new students but was amazed to find a college professor, economist and a dentist in the earlier class.

After being introduced to the class and telling them a little about myself, my job was to check their homework and answer questions. Although most were tired from working all day, their enthusiasm and eagerness to learn was infectious. No deadbeats in this class.

George presented current events, vocabulary and additional individual written work throughout the evening. As I sat there I was struck by the difference in this class and many classrooms in regular elementary and secondary schools. There was no competition. Everyone was there to learn and help each other. Each student had the opportunity to read out loud and when they made a mistake in pronunciation everyone hooted and laughed—but not at the reader—they were laughing with him.

Neither George nor I were sure of the spelling of "inauguration" when he wrote it on the blackboard. About fifteen minutes later a huge man with laborer's hands raised his hand. He was excited because he had searched diligently and found the correct spelling in his Portuguese dictionary. A coup. The hero of the evening. Everyone laughed and applauded, including George.

No females afraid to answer any questions because they might be considered "too brainy". No one afraid to raise his hand and possibly give an incorrect answer with the fear of being teased. No one afraid to touch my sleeve and ask for help although it was the first time he met me.

Imagine if this ease, sense of common goals and feeling of community could be replicated in classrooms throughout our country. I realize these are completely different circumstances, but just think of how many happy students would troop into class each day, ego intact and unafraid to learn.

September 2000

EARRINGS

Too expensive, can't afford them
although no price is known
Don't belong in this shop of treasures—but

On white satin—created for me
two triangles of hope and joy
held by slender silver hooks

Aqua, pink, amethyst
stones cascading down a waterfall
reflecting beauty and promise
of new life and a future
of harmony, splendor and elegance
for a withered soul.

1999

JUST LIKE YOUR MOTHER

Words intended as a kind and affirming compliment—"you look just like your mother"—instead have often made countless women cringe and shake their heads in silent disagreement. Unfortunately for many, it's the last thing they want to hear.

When I was a little girl, whenever someone said that to me I felt wonderful. I thought my mom was beautiful and wanted to be just like her. But as I grew older and began to realize that she had some traits I didn't appreciate, I started to resent hearing those words. I didn't want to look like or be like my mom. I wanted to be me. But I always smiled and said "thank you" because I didn't want to hurt her feelings.

I remember a day when I was in my late thirties and had bought a new winter hat. My hair was already gray but the bangs which framed my face were almost white. I looked in the mirror and was horrified. The hat covered all of my hair except the bangs. Between the hat, the white fringe covering my forehead and the large, unfashionable eye-glasses I wore at the time, I looked about fifteen years older and *exactly like my mother*. I dyed my hair blonde the next day.

Every once in a while I caught a glimpse of myself in a mirror or a store window—shoulders slumped forward, forehead furrowed, an angry curl to my lip—*exactly like my mother*. I would immediately straighten up and plaster a smile on my face. It was only after my dad died that slowly mom and I became closer. I had finally grown up, understanding her for the first time, and was able to let go of the resentment I felt toward her since I was a child. During the seven years she lived in a senior citizen housing complex before her death, her friends often greeted me with "darling, you look just like your mom". It was a wonderful feeling to say "thank you" and finally mean it.

So you would think I would be more aware of a daughter's feelings when I had my own child. But I wasn't. Nancy was born when her brothers were eight and six and our family was thrilled and delighted with her arrival. As she grew up, the inevitable comparisons were made between mother and daughter. "She looks exactly like you", friends and strangers would tell us. I was so proud. But I made sure to mention that Nancy had curly hair while mine was straight. Or that she had hazel eyes and mine were blue. She needed her own identity, not her mom's. I thought I had taken care of the problem.

Then one night when she was about seven, I was tucking her into bed after we had had a family birthday party. As usual, many guests had commented how much Nancy and I looked alike. She looked up at me and started to cry. "What's the matter honey, what happened?" "I don't want to hurt your feelings, mommy." "Come on Nance; it's ok to tell me why you're upset." "I love you so much mommy but I don't want to look like you." She started to sob as I held her in my arms. "Everybody says I look just like you. But you have gray hair, and eyeglasses and wrinkles and those brown spots on your hands and face. You look old." She cried harder. Dear God, that's what she thought people saw when they looked at her. Who can ever truly know what their child is thinking or feeling?

Hugging her tightly, I tried to reassure her, explaining what people meant when they said someone looked like another person: perhaps the shape of their eyes, or they smiled the same way, or they had the same hair color. She looked at me warily. "Do they see my curly hair and that it's brown?" "Of course they do Nan." "And that I don't have wrinkles and spots on my face?" "No, honey, you have beautiful skin." She smiled a little. "Will I always look like me, mommy?" Sure you will honey. When you get older you'll look like a teenager and then like a young lady, but you'll always look like you." "You're not mad that I don't want to look like you, mommy?" "Not for a minute, honey." "Ok, I feel better. I think I can go to sleep now."

My daughter is now twenty-nine. Still, often when we're together, someone mentions that we look alike. I don't hear her protest and hope that as she carries herself with grace, joy and self-assurance she enjoys who she is, knowing she is Nancy, not her mom.

October 2003

BLACK STOCKINGS

Age 5-12—St. Michael's Elementary School. Sister David roughly pulls back my shoulders. "Sit up straight like a lady. You never listen." Ugly, heavy, patched black stockings cover her legs. What do they wear underneath?—A good Catholic girl

Age 13-18—St. Mary's High School—"Get that smirk off your face. Try and act like a lady for a change. I don't see much hope for you anyway." Black cotton stockings droop around Sister Agnes' fat ankles. Do they ever think about sex? Each night in bed I hide beneath the covers, flashlight in hand praying penitential prayers listed in my "Catholic Girls Guide". I seek forgiveness for I know I am dammed to hell if I die the next day because of perceived impure thoughts and behaviors.—A good Catholic girl.

Age 20-30—New bride. Rhythm method of birth control. "We can't. It's not the right time. Don't come near me." Blouses still button to the top and slacks and skirts fit loosely.—A good Catholic girl.

Age 30-50—Wife, mother, daughter. Three children, full time job, sick parents. "I'm tired. Try taking care of everything around here and working all day and you'd be tired too. I'm going to sleep." Business suits, gray stockings.—A good Catholic girl.

Age 50-60—Night sweats, mood swings, sagging breasts, stomach and eyelids. One big lump. "I'm sorry I hurt your feelings but I can't wear this sexy teddy. I feel like a cow." A good Catholic girl.

Age 60+—Retired, refreshed, renewed. "Hey honey. I'm wearing black silky stockings, spike heels, lipstick, earrings and "Obsession". I'm ready." A good Catholic girl.

March 2000

TED WILLIAMS

The news regarding Ted Williams' heart surgery the past few days brought back memories of the one time I saw him play, a day I'll never forget. My team was the Brooklyn Dodgers, forever trying to win, or even qualify for the World Series. I hated the New York Yankees with a passion because they never lost. For years it seemed as if they had nine players in their lineup who could hit a winning home run at the bottom of the ninth inning in every game they played. Relief pitchers didn't have a chance.

My father was a New York Giants fan but his employer, Prudential Insurance, sponsored a bus trip to the Yankee-Red Sox double header so we went. Dad would never drive to New York; he stayed close to home. One of his heroes was Dominic Di Maggio who played for the Red Sox and he knew I loved Ted Williams so I guess he was giving us both a treat. My brother tagged along, not really interested, but not wanting to be left out.

The entrances to the stadium were packed. Once inside we slowly followed the crowd toward our seats in the upper tier along the first base line. I passed through the turnstile, stepped through the passage and got my first view of the "House That Ruth Built". The immense expanse of Yankee Stadium was filled to capacity with cheering fans. Brilliant green grass stretched as far as I could see; the brick red dirt, white-lined infield and bases sparkled in the sun. Straight ahead in center field the American flag stood out against a pale blue sky. It was magic.

I don't remember much about the games except that I cheered wildly each time Ted Williams came to bat. Pictures of him were scotch-taped all over my bedroom walls along with those of Johnny Unitas, who was the quarterback for the Baltimore Colts. Williams was a great player, brash, often not a favorite of reporters and sometimes not even of the fans or his teammates. He was his own person and answered to no one. Only as I grew older I realized it was probably this aspect of his personality that appealed to me most.

Because our seats were on the first base line, when Williams, a lefty, came up to bat I had a perfect picture of his style and being a lefty I could gain tips from watching him. I was so in awe that I was really watching Ted Williams I sat transfixed. Then he hit a game-winning home run in the first game. A fluid, powerful swing, the crack of the bat and he loped around the bases. Yelling like crazy, I jumped up and down until my dad gently pulled me back into my seat.

It seemed like a long time between games but the wait was worth it. The first time up in the second game he hit a home run. The score was tied when he came to bat in the ninth inning. He hit another home run which put Boston ahead. I couldn't believe it. Now the Yankees were up and I clenched my hands, biting my nails and peeking through my fingers. Which Yankee would hit the home runs today which would tie the score and then win the game?

No one did. Three outs—1-2-3. What else is there to say?

January 2001

TERROR

I'm upset that I seemed to lack any depth of feeling in the first days after the terrorist attacks. I always thought terrorists would attack our country one day in some horrible way, but never something like this. Bush's image on television—the poor man. God please help him. I turned off the set when they listed the dead along with their photos. Why was I unwilling or unable to share the pain these families felt? I hated the detachment and denial which seemed to be my strongest coping skills at that point. That wasn't me. Or was it?

A few days after the disaster my daughter, who is twenty-six and lives with me and who has tried to forge a life for herself on Cape Cod for the last three years, told her employer she would be moving back to New Jersey when he was able to find someone to replace her. "I just sat there, mom, looking at that television screen asked myself: why are you sitting here wasting your life when you have so much to offer, so much you want to do and you know you can't have the life you want here." Terror and the realization of how fragile life is gave her the courage to take a step forward to a new beginning.

One of my first reactions was God had allowed this for a reason none of us can know or understand but that in some way good will come from it. I felt in my heart that our society has been drifting away from the true meaning of life slowly for many years. The need to be first, have the most and "be connected" all the time has only fractured and fragmented families and it doesn't seem to make folks happier in any way I can see.

With the desperate need we seem to have to be first, I've always wondered who would be willing to get in line in second place. In my blue-collar hometown in New Jersey there's constant competition among adults to own the most expensive car, wear more gold or buy a larger home. In the resort town in Massachusetts where our retirement home is located, this summer many obviously wealthy families, both summer residents and those on vacation, seemed more hostile and impatient and rarely smiled. I wonder—what will make us happy?

A week after the attacks I returned to my home in New Jersey for week's visit and the tragedy became more real. A friend's son had taken a job at the World Trade Center three weeks before the attack but had missed the train that day.

Another friend's son escaped from one of the towers. Why did I feel more comfortable and secure among the crowded, diverse population in my town of 52,000 than I had while sitting alone at Harding's Beach on Cape Cod?

I looked through the newspaper list for the name of someone I knew among the thirty-two who were missing from my town but fortunately found none. My dentist told me that twenty fathers and mothers of young children who lived in his town didn't make it. How do I understand this? I watched as the New York Mets honored all those in pain in unforgettable ceremonies before the first baseball game played in New York since the tragedy.

My home in New Jersey is located fifteen minutes from Newark Liberty International Airport and thirty minutes from Manhattan. At times, according to wind direction, the take-off flight plan directs many planes at extremely low altitudes over my home. It was cloudy all week so I was unable to see any of them until this morning. Only then, when I saw a jumbo-jet soaring low overhead could I start to feel the terror of September 11th. Later, after lunch my husband I decided to go shopping. The highway entrance we use to get to the mall affords a marvelous view of the Twin Towers less than twenty miles away. Today there was nothing to see.

9-21-01

NOVEMBER GARDENS

I just came into the house after roaming around in what's left of our garden and felt sad that another season had passed. I remembered the last garden I had cleared out in November, my dad's. He had died the month before and I wanted it to be cleaned up for the fall as he would have done. A bleak season. But then today after lunch I took a second look at the scraggly plants and withered stalks outside my kitchen door and found joy instead of sadness.

My daughter, Nancy, was the major gardener in our family this year and I saw her everywhere. In the decaying pots of herbs she had grown from seed and proudly incorporated in her cooking through the summer. In the yellow and green rotting tomatoes which had fallen on the ground, hidden beneath the foliage and now a snack for raccoons who visit us nightly. She had planted the tomatoes from seed in early spring and nurtured them as she would a child. Her perennials—a wide variety of flowering plants and bushes, roses and Black-Eyed Susans were hunkering down for the winter.

On the hill behind the deck she had planted a variety of ground-covers, some with bright purple flowers, some red, others covered with tiny white stars. They were now creeping across the walk, still in full bloom, reaching for the freedom of the woods and bog beyond. As she is now ready to reach for freedom and new life.

Chronic depression has been a constant companion for many years. She has lived in our home in New Jersey and on the Cape at various intervals, trying to find her way. God has been kind and she is ready to soar. Her mind is clear and open to a new world. She is vibrantly alive when she returns from one of the evening college courses she's taking. She grins and chatters endlessly about her classes and the joy of learning. For the first time in her life she realizes that she is an extremely bright, gifted woman and the world is hers.

Her gift to me was love and perspective. I always knew the love was there but her perspective and insight into who I am and where I am in life right now were amazing. As she said, "Gee ma, sometimes I feel like you're my kid". That's not a good place for a child to be. I am at my own crossroads in life with many decisions to be made. She shook the cobwebs, resentment and anger out of my brain, heart and soul and filled them with her love, knowledge and compassion.

Her signature favorite sunflowers have almost all withered. A few of the plants have been uprooted by wind. But today I picked two that were left on the stalks—one a Van Gogh yellow, the other glorious orange. Now they rest in a tankard on my kitchen windowsill, a reminder that although Nancy will be leaving, the joy of who she is will always fill our home.

November 2001

MIGHTY DUCK

Mighty Duck is flying in two directions as he always does. It's not easy. I've tried it for ages and it just doesn't work. Years ago my husband's friend presented him with a duck for our home on Cape Cod. This is a special species of duck, able to flap separate wings in opposite directions at the same time. I don't understand the mechanics, but however the metal wings are attached to the gray and white wooden body, it allows the unique creature to fly in two directions at once.

My husband couldn't wait to give the duck a home and wanted him to fly high atop a pole attached to the fence on our front lawn. Totally tacky I protested. He wasn't amused and consigned the poor bird to the garage for years. This summer, however, I was surprised to see him (the duck) flying atop a small metal pole attached to the top of the arbor in our backyard. He flew valiantly in the every-present breeze, oblivious to the brilliant morning glories which danced on the arbor beneath him.

I pretty much ignored the bird's flight until one cool morning this summer as I sat on the deck having a cup of coffee after breakfast. I was in a funk and having a hard time shaking it. The bright sunshine, flowers and birds at the feeder did not lift my mood. Then I saw the duck whirling away and started to laugh. I saw my life.

The poised duck awaits flight, brown-spotted wings lined up evenly. One wing starts spinning slowly while the other remains motionless. Then it stops and reverses. The pole moves slightly and both wings spin wildly in the breeze—in opposite directions. The pole shifts again; one wing slows to a stop as the other increases its speed. Slowly, it continues to travel in circles. On rare occasions both wings will line up exactly and even start to spin in the same direction, but only for a few seconds. Sometimes both wings are tilted forward, other times both tilt backward. Which way am I going?

I live on Cape Cod; I live in New Jersey. Health is good; health is poor. Family is happy; family's a disaster. Plans are made for a day, a week, a month. Then life intrudes and plans, hopes and dreams are changed or set aside. The longer I watch the duck flapping away, the harder I laugh. "Going in circles, which end is up, pulled in two directions"—how many more clichés describe my feathered friend? I've often described much of my life as controlled chaos and although I laugh as often as I can, I don't always think it's funny. But my duck brilliantly reminds me that emotional ventures in many directions—travels throughout a lifetime—are a fate which I share with many others.

Today—another funk. Having friends for dinner and I've lost the tablecloth. Can't find it anywhere. How do you lose a tablecloth? I need a haircut and my toenail polish is chipped beyond repair. Really important problems.

Then my husband returns from the post office and sets the mail on the counter. It includes Newsweek's commemorative issue for September 11th. My son calls to say a promised loan to expand his business is now in jeopardy. My daughter flies out of the house to drive a friend to Cape Cod Hospital to be with her child who has just attempted suicide. I learn a friend is scheduled for immediate cancer surgery.

Upset and despondent, I step onto the deck to search the sky for Mighty Duck. For I am sure that as he flies to far destinations, he will be able to provide balance, perspective and remind me once again that life will be ok.

August 2002

HIBISCUS

Will Kevin succeed in his new job? Will Chris finally get the financing for the business? Will Nancy get the job she applied for today? Thoughts of my children whirl around in my head as I sit down for a cup of tea at the kitchen table. Adult children who can take care of themselves. But when you love, how do you stop worrying about them, stop waiting for them to be "settled"?

As I sit at the table, my eyes wander toward the large hibiscus plant on the floor next to me. Gazing at the glory of the scarlet flower which opened this morning and thinking about its brief life cycle, I remember again God's perfect order in nature, proof of His design in our lives—a reminder life happens in His time, not mine.

The hibiscus bud forms slowly, swelling to become a pink embryo which is born one glorious morning in shades of crimson and yellow. It lives a full life in this one day, dancing in the sunlight and bringing joy. I nod and smile each time I gently touch it, acknowledging the peace with which it fills me. Then it rests overnight, still in full bloom.

The following morning, imperceptibly, one at a time, the five petals start to slowly turn back inward toward their core. It is this gradual folding inward of each petal that again reminds me to try to see and accept life on a daily basis without worrying about the future. I'm aware as I pass the plant through the course of the day that not all petals close at the same pace, as the stages of different lives are not measured evenly. We come into the world full of life and promise. The years progress and we become all we can be by filling our days yet always reaching toward the next. Then, aging slowly, we turn inward as gently as the petal turns inward to rest.

Another night passes and in the morning the bud has slipped off its stem and rests on the floor. I pick it up and notice how tightly the petals have closed around each other, their job finished. Gently I set it in the yard under oak leaves so it may return to the earth.

6-8-02

THE ODD COUPLE

We trudged across the cranberry bog carrying our buckets, large plastic bags to kneel on, rags, gloves, a thermos and sandwiches. Olive was always prepared for any contingency. At eighty she had more energy and gumption than I could muster on a good day. I had been trying to match her pace ever since I had met her five years ago.

"Big ones in here," she said, spreading her bag on the ground and kneeling down. I settled next to her on the thick mass of vines. She showed me how to shape my fingers to rake out the fruit and pretty soon I was filling my pail with bright red berries. I liked the crunch of the stiff green vines as my fingers groped cautiously searching for clumps of berries hidden in the thicket. The earth smelled fresh and pure and the salt air blowing over the ridge from the bay soothed my soul.

Olive bent over, ripping at vines along a trough. "We'll get lots today; the machines they used for the harvest didn't do a good job this year." I looked at my friend, delighted again that we had met each other. She, the reticent New Englander proud of her Yankee heritage hadn't quite known what to do with this volatile Italian New Jersey retiree.

We met in a writing class when I moved to Cape Cod from New Jersey. Slowly and tentatively we reached out in friendship. Olive was an accomplished musician, teacher, writer and artist whom I admired tremendously. At first she responded to my often emotional conversations with a quizzical look, slight grin or silence. Puzzled by her response, I sometimes mistook her silence for lack of interest or disapproval. But as we spent more time together attending plays, lectures or going on nature walks and shared our stories and lives, we became friends. Her slow, patient manner helped temper my impulsiveness. And now I can give her a big hug and receive one in return.

We worked in companionable silence beneath the unseasonably warm November sun. Sentinels of ragged pines and maples dressed in gold lined the bog. A huge variety of birds chattered joyfully, hawks circled overhead and seagulls swept past headed toward the bay for lunch.

After a break for a sandwich and drink, we returned to our work with our buckets only half-full. Born and raised on Cape Cod, Olive described her happy life growing up, remembering how she had picked berries with her dad at this same bog. "Before the tourists got here," she smiled. She laughed often, relating the adventures of many generations of her New England ancestors. I had taken a step back in time and felt sad that I knew so little about my own ancestors and their history.

"Ok, guess it's time to pack up. Doesn't look like we'll get much more today." It was late afternoon; the sun had retreated behind gathering clouds and the wind from the bay had gotten much stronger. Olive held up her bucket. "Looks like I might have a few more than you do," she teased. I grinned back at her, acknowledging her superior berry-picking skills and the joy she had brought me this glorious fall day.

November 2002

FULL CIRCLE

Since my father had married in a Catholic ceremony and was then divorced, by marrying my mom he was ex-communicated from the church. As a child I could never understand this because he was such a good and kind man and it didn't seem fair. At weekly mass as I knelt next to him, I was in awe at the reverence I felt emanate from him. How could he pray so fervently I wondered, if the church didn't even accept him as a member.

As I grew up I questioned and became less accepting of the church and its rules. They seemed to be mostly man-made rules that had little to do with God, spirituality or becoming a good person. But I continued to struggle with my feelings, becoming more involved with the church as a Eucharistic Minister, attending many home-based group discussion meetings and helping plan parish social functions. I hoped they would bring me closer to a true acceptance of my faith.

I took a three year course to become a lay minister in my parish so I could more actively participate in ritual and also bring comfort to those who were hurting. Another woman from my parish was also taking the course with me at a nearby parish on the same night. Our daughters had gone through school together and had played on the same junior and senior high softball teams and we had often car-pooled over the years. Whenever I waved to her during our class breaks she ignored me and refused to acknowledge my greeting. She chose not to know me. Why? I have no idea. Neither did many of my classmates seem to practice Christian ideals and often couldn't even be tolerant of each other's differing opinions during class discussions. Everyone wanted to be in charge. I wondered more than ever what religion was all about.

My dad became ill and was at home dying from cancer. More than anything he wanted to receive communion and the last rites of the church. Father Brian from our parish came to see him and my dad told him his story of being ex-communicated. Father Brian gave dad communion every day during the month before he died. He gave him the last rites and I know my dad died a happy and peaceful man.

At the end of my lay ministry course, after learning much of the history of the church and how it had evolved over the centuries, I knew I could no longer participate in mass and practice a faith which I felt was so hypocritical. Without guilt, I stopped going to mass. I heard that Father Brian was transferred to a distant parish since he had many disagreements with his pastor.

This past weekend I went to New Jersey for my grandson's christening. My son's family lives in the same parish I used to belong to. Their pastor explained he could not baptize the baby because the godparents didn't meet the parish's criteria. My daughter-in-law visited a neighboring parish whose pastor gave permission for the baptism. She said the pastor seemed to be a kind and understanding man.

As the pastor walked into church to start the ceremony, imagine my amazement to see Father Brian once again after twenty-seven years. He baptized my grandson. I spoke to him after the ceremony to thank him and mentioned that this was the second time he had brought great joy to my life. We shared again the days he had visited my father at home and the peace and acceptance my dad felt by receiving communion from him. He is truly a man of God.

October 2002

MOTHER'S DAY

My daughter lives on the Cape near me but the rest of my family was in New Jersey for Mother's Day. That's fine because I'm not one of those moms who need all their children around every birthday or holiday. I remember feeling obligated and torn between which families to visit for each holiday after I got married and swore I would never do that to my kids. I know they love me and we have a deep connection and that's what counts.

My husband called with lots of love and was going to work in the yard in New Jersey planting flowers—that was a great gift. My older son and his family phoned during their breakfast with lots of love to send me on my way through the day. My daughter took me to Bonnat's for breakfast where we had a marvelous chat. She gave me a deep blue, crackled glass ball to hang in my kitchen window and a small kitchen ornament which says "Live Well—Laugh Often—Love Much"—perfect.

I returned a call from my younger son when I got home and got my daughter-in-law on the phone. We are developing a close and warm relationship and I am blessed. My two grandsons were kicking up a fuss in the background so we didn't talk long. "I want you to know you got two cards—one from the family and one from Chris alone since he picked out the "from your son" card and said it was perfect for you," she told me. She could probably see me grinning. I haven't gotten a card like that from him in years and when it arrived the other day it confirmed feelings I know exist and never change.

Nancy's boyfriend's family had invited me for dinner. I had met his parents once and shared a short conversation with them but this would be our first time together for any length of time. I had to make sure I was on good behavior since I tend to say what I mean—sometimes without thinking—and didn't want to embarrass Nancy. "Oh, ma—just be yourself", she scolded.

We spent a lovely afternoon. It was nice to be "company" and not worry about family dynamics, instead sitting back to enjoy the interactions of another family. Is there anything more interesting than watching people? They made me feel comfortable and it was easy to be with the many relatives who were visiting. A few water glasses were knocked over at the table before we sat down; there was disagreement on how long to leave the meat in the oven; kids fussed over who would sit at the adult table; the mushrooms and onions started to burn in the frying pan; eyebrows raised and eyeballs rolled toward heaven. It was wonderful. I felt like I was home.

May 2003

MANHATTAN CHRISTMAS

It's a week before Christmas and I'm seated on a bus with my husband and our friends, Bob and Carol, heading into Manhattan to view "the tree" at Rockefeller Center. There is much to see outside my window. The glow of Newark Airport on the right and acres of blazing red tail-lights to the left form a mosaic of motion. The variety of lights of New York and New Jersey fascinate me as always; luminous pearls are strung across bridges connecting to the magic island. They obliterate the somber, soggy marshland which borders the turnpike.

I can't take my eyes away from the Empire State Building because if I do I'll see the void where the Trade Towers stood. Somehow tonight the emptiness is worse than the scenes of destruction on September 11th. As we head for the Lincoln Tunnel entrance, the elegant skyline across the river appears as if a stage prop and mesmerizes me as it always does.

We wait in one of ten lines of traffic that will filter into two to proceed through the tunnel. I see a sign that says "Class B Explosives Prohibited". Christmas, a tunnel, terrorists. I'm ashamed that my throat tightens in fear for a moment until I shake off the feeling, remembering that I cannot live in fear, for that is not living. A solitary man is outlined in the window of the Port Authority office high above the traffic, pacing slowly back and forth while we wait. Does he have a magic screen that tells him when midtown traffic starts to ease, a magic button to push to allow us to enter the tunnel? Moments later the bus starts to move and I'm impressed that this traffic flows smoothly on a daily basis.

The city is packed with tourists, shoppers and endless lines of tour buses similar to ours. I marvel at the way our driver maneuvers down the narrow cross streets. We pause for a light near Broadway and I'm disappointed that the character of this area has been replaced by a Disney-like façade. Signs and displays are uniformly gaudy—too large, bright and glitzy. Bigger and brighter doesn't mean better.

We hop off the bus and head for Rockefeller Center a few blocks away. I taste and feel the energy of the city. The sidewalks are so packed I sense that if I lift my feet off the ground, I will be carried along by the momentum of others. This feeling would have terrified me years ago; tonight it is exhilarating. I am surprised to see countless young couples with toddlers in strollers or riding on their parents' shoulders. Most people are smiling.

The tree. But something's wrong. It's too small, not bright enough. Then I realize we have approached the tree from the rear, not from the promenade which leads up to the front of it. Folks in Santa suits are speaking numerous languages, encouraging visitors to have their photos taken in front of the tree. Santa snaps our photo and a minute later I see myself—someone giddy and laughing—who is truly enjoying life.

We round the corner and approach the tree from the front. The mezzanine is lined on both sides by gigantic toy soldiers covered with tiny white lights which remind me of stars. Now the tree is magic—tall, full and glorious—enveloped in a waterfall of colorful lights, a gleaming star at the top. Crushed by the crowd we try to re-trace our steps but the smiling policeman informs. us this is a "one way only sidewalk" so we follow the crowd to a place where we can breathe again.

I hear a woman asking a policeman if she is indeed looking at the Empire State Building. "Lady, where ya lookin—I can't see anything." Apparently his view is obstructed so she tries to point it out to him. He's directing traffic but attempts to be patient as he bobs and ducks looking for the building. She regards him with dismay, how can he not know? After a moment he says, "Gee lady, I'm sorry I don't really know, I live in the Bronx."

On our way to the restaurant we pass St. Patrick's Cathedral. It is bathed in the same white light which illuminates it every evening but tonight the cathedral doesn't look majestic; it looks eerie, almost menacing. And I wonder—is it reflective of the state of the Catholic Church in America today?

We enter the restaurant and I'm assaulted by loud, raucous music and conversation. I'm getting old I guess because this Irish pub bar scene is not my idea of a night out. Luckily the waitress seats us at a table in the front, far from the holiday celebrants. The pub was forced to move from a previous location near Times Square and has lost much of its charm, now decorated with gaudy plastic leprechauns and neon shamrocks. The men question the waitress about the disparity in prices between the regular menu and the daily special sheet she has handed us. She explains that these are new prices just starting today—"holiday prices" she smiles. Our husbands have a lengthy discussion with the waitress regarding the change, finally acknowledging they have to pay $2 more for each entrée. Eyes rolling and nodding to each other, Carol and I change our drink order from soda to wine—we'll need it.

Later, on the way to the ladies' room we run a gauntlet between wary, vacant-eyed patrons jammed against the bar and a crush of mostly young revelers with darting eyes who are pushed together against the opposite wall. Hardly anyone looks happy and I'm thankful I'm an old married lady and not part of today's dating scene. Two bleary-eyed women stumble into me. A man clutches a beer bottle, frenetically searching for something, someone. He spots a stool at the end of the bar and hunches forward, curling into himself.

Back at the table as I sit across from Bob and Carol I realize once again how lucky I am to have them as friends. We've shared a friendship of over thirty years and it's a great feeling to know they're always there to count on. We've finished dinner and our wine has provided a rosy glow. Pretty soon it's time to leave.

Back outside after a delicious meal, we head back to the bus. The air is much colder but feels good against my flushed face. Our four hours in Manhattan are up and we must return home. My visit leaves me feeling refreshed and renewed but wistful for more. I know I'll be back next year.

December 2003

AFFIRMATION

For almost a year I thought any creativity I had within me had died. Everything I wrote sounded like something from a first grade reader—"See the dog run; see the dog run fast". Over the years I've had many dry periods when I couldn't write anything but never for this long. And I couldn't figure out why. I was happy, healthy, not in one of my emotional funks; my family was fairly peaceful. I couldn't write in New Jersey, but neither could I write at the Cape.

I've always preached to my kids that everything in life happens in God's time, not our time; that we just have to keep trying and........wait. But this time I sure wasn't listening to myself. I was upset, full of despair and felt empty. And then, along with the spring rains came a cleansing of my mind. Slowly at first but then like a deluge, ideas, feelings and stories filled my head and heart and I couldn't get them down on paper fast enough. Why? How? I have no idea and have finally learned to stop asking since I never get an answer.

Then this week came. A magical week when the mail, e-mail and a phone call all brought affirmation to me as a writer: a copy of "Personal Journaling" magazine which includes my short piece on the bravery of my mom and mother-in-law as they both faced death from terminal cancer at the same time. An acceptance from a small writer's newsletter on the subject of "my first sale" which was an inspirational piece about my son sent it to Catholic Digest twenty-five years ago. It was then picked up and re-printed by The National Enquirer—twice.

A letter accepting a poem, "Arranging Gladiolus", which is about trying to make a marriage work, to be published in a poetry anthology for Christmas. Two essays about summer on the Cape when my kids were youngsters will be printed in an online magazine, "Philosophical Mother", in July and August. The editor offered me my own column which now appears monthly.

I had one of my pieces included in "A Sense of Place", an anthology of Cape Cod women writers which was published last fall. Wendy Levine of the Payomet Theater in Truro called me this week. In July, actors will be reading selections from "A Sense of Place" and she wanted permission to include "Black Stockings" in the program.

I feel successful as a writer because my words are being shared. I never expected to make any money from writing and I never will. When I deduct the cost of postage, paper and the books of mine bought from publishers to give to friends and family, I'm sure running at a huge loss. But I'm sharing. Perhaps making someone happier, helping them to look at a problem from a new point of view or bringing laughter to their day.

June 2003

FIFTY YEARS AGO

Fifty years ago. Could that really be? Was it truly fifty years ago as an eighth grade student that I sat at a table in this school cafeteria? Yes indeed. The realization jolts me at first but then I am filled with a sense of joy. Some of the happiest years of my life were spent in Washington School, days filled with warmth, laughter and accomplishment. Today I am part of the school's "Special Friends and Relatives Day", there as a representative to visit the classroom of my nine-year old neighbor, Gabbby. Neither of her parents could take off from work and I am thrilled to be asked to visit.

As I sit there watching the PTA moms serve coffee and cake to the guests, I remember the days I had been the PTA room representative for my three kids as they passed through the grades at Washington School. It had been a marvelous feeling for me to have my children attend the same school I did, although PTA members quibbling over inane things like the icing color on holiday cookies was sure not for me. But we did our duty as mothers.

My town has changed. When I was growing up in Union, it consisted mainly of German families and Mayor Biertuempfel was the father figure, holding office for over thirty years. Present town politics remain a struggle among competing factions. Today the diversity of the town is reflected in the multi-hued complexions and varied languages of the visitors sitting at my table waiting to visit the classrooms.

I look out the cafeteria window at the playground and the flood of memories is astounding. Would Tommy pick me for his team at lunchtime? Would he chase me around the playground during tag tomorrow to show me he really liked me? Remembering the gawky, (string bean and lizard legs were my nicknames) shy girl who worked so hard to make him notice me makes me laugh out loud.

I lived only two blocks from the school so my mom made me come home for lunch every day. I hated it because it took away from playground time with the popular kids who ate in the cafeteria. On the way back from lunch, I would leap over the garbage cans placed at the curb in front of each home but it didn't slow me down. Considered one of the best girl athletes at school, I had to stay in shape.

After greetings from the principal, we make our way to the classrooms. Past the principal's office where a few teachers sent me because of "that sassy mouth of yours".

Past the nurse's office where she would call my mom—"Please come and get Gerry; she's sick again". Past the auditorium where I linger a long time, watching a group of kids singing joyfully, preparing for a spring musical program. I remember standing on the stage for the first time in third grade, scared to death and sick to my stomach, holding a huge, white cardboard goose. I was Mother Goose and center stage in our third grade production. It's difficult to leave the auditorium since visions of rainy day movies, special magic shows once a year, Christmas productions and award assemblies fly through my mind. I received many academic and athletic awards on that stage at a time in my life when I really felt like I was somebody and could conquer the world.

Gabby's huge grin greets me as I enter her fourth grade classroom and take a seat at the desk next to her. Posters, games, puzzles and plants line the shelves and windowsills. Colorful mobiles hanging from the ceiling sway in the spring breeze filtering through the windows. Her teacher's bright smile and enthusiasm are infectious.

After the teacher reviews curriculum highlights for the year, the students each read a letter to their visitor explaining what that person means to them. A few mention they are thankful for gifts of money or toys they've received but the majority of them surprise me by thanking their family and friends and emphasizing what matters: "comfort, love, help, understanding, you don't holler, reading a book together, helping me with my homework, going shopping together, snuggling to watch television and going for a walk". The love and depth of affection expressed by the students was wonderful. Friends and family seem surprised by the letters and many have tears in their eyes as they listen.

Gabby gives me a big hug goodbye and it is time to leave. I hate to go. To sit in a classroom for a few hours with a vibrant, caring teacher, watching children excited by learning is the most life-affirming experience I've had in a long time. These are children who know they are special and are eager to embrace life and all it has to offer.

3-18-03

MOST OF THE TIME

Ever since I was a young child all I remember being told is to sit down and be quiet, keep your mouth shut because no one cares about your opinions, girls should be seen and not heard and talk like a lady. I remember being chased by my mom or dad after I had sassed them back, always wanting to have the last word. I wanted to share me but no one wanted to listen.

I filled countless secret diaries, recorded pages of fantasy, dreams and hopes in a collection of rainbow-colored spiral notebooks and had opinions about everything. Strong opinions, usually contrary to popular opinion. Why couldn't they see that just because everyone thought the same way it didn't necessarily make it right? You were entitled to your opinion but I would try my darndest to make you see my way. I took great pride in "telling it like it is".

I loved sharing ideas and philosophies and others often sought me out for understanding or advice. Joyce Brothers of the telephone is how my husband referred to me for many years, not always kindly. And I wrote—notes, letters, essays, a newspaper column. To my family I was the nudge, often the nag. They didn't realize I thought I was guiding them, helping them see the way.

Too often I reacted emotionally to situations and responded inappropriately. The brain went into gear and either hurtful comments or words which would later come back to haunt me shot out of my mouth. Or traveled from my brain down to fingers which recorded many words which were not always kind.

Only by listening, watching and absorbing how my children relate to their friends and families the last few years have I learned what an unkind and impulsive tongue I often possessed. As I watched my son discipline his two toddlers in a strong but kind manner, I realized I had frequently used much harsher language raising my children and often did not treat them with respect. I wanted to protest to my older son when I felt his boss or a new friend was taking advantage of his cheerful and always-willing-to-help nature but realized I should keep my mouth shut. It's not my business. I always meant well and assumed I was "helping" my adult children with my comments and suggestions. But isn't the road to hell paved with good intentions? My daughter's gentle reminders of "that's the way daddy is" revealed my husband in a new light and forced me to re-think and I hope strongly improve my relationship with him in many ways.

And a child shall lead them. And they did. I actually wait to be asked for advice now (most of the time); I watch family interactions and disputes without comment (most of the time); I smile and nod when my husband is spouting off rather than offering my opinion (most of the time). I'm getting there. Come on over for coffee. We'll talk.

Spring 2003

0-595-31249-7

Printed in the United States
30935LVS00004B/187-234

9 780595 312498